W9-DHF-683

The continuing development of automated production methods, combined with increasing competition in manufactures from low-wage developing economies, is likely to reduce yet further the scope for the employment of low skilled and inexperienced personnel in advanced economies if Britain is to benefit from advanced technology. Higher standards of schooling and of vocational training are now widely recognised as essential in Britain – as in the United States and many other industrialised countries. This book provides a realistic analysis of what needs to be done, based on visits by expert teams to matched samples of manufacturing plants, as well as to schools and vocational colleges in Britain and Continental Europe.

The policy emphasis derived from these studies is on the need to expand, not the proportion of the workforce with university qualifications, but those with craft and vocational qualifications. Concern with schooling attainments and the focus of school curricula need to be shifted towards helping those of average ability – though not at the expense of the most able who have for long been exceptionally well served by the British educational system.

The author has headed a team of researchers at the National Institute of Economic and Social Research (London) who have been engaged in international comparisons in this field for the past ten years. Their findings have been influential in the development of government policies in this area. This book represents the first comprehensive account of their findings; it explains why government policies need to move even further, and in which directions those policies must next move.

THE NATIONAL INSTITUTE OF
ECONOMIC AND SOCIAL RESEARCH

Occasional Papers
XLVIII

PRODUCTIVITY, EDUCATION AND TRAINING
An international perspective

PRODUCTIVITY, EDUCATION AND TRAINING
An international perspective

S. J. PRAIS

CAMBRIDGE
UNIVERSITY PRESS

Published by the Press Syndicate of the University of Cambridge
The Pitt Building, Trumpington Street, Cambridge CB2 1RP
40 West 20th Street, New York, NY 10011-4211, USA
10 Stamford Road, Oakleigh, Melbourne 3166, Australia

First published 1995

Printed in Great Britain at the University Press, Cambridge

A *catalogue record for this book is available from the British Library*

Library of Congress cataloguing in publication data

Prais, S. J.
    Productivity, education and training: an international perspective / S. J. Prais
    p. cm.– (Occasional papers / National Institute of Economic and Social
Research: 48)
    Includes bibliographical references and index.
    ISBN 0 521 48305 0
    1. Occupational training – Great Britain. 2. Vocational education – Great Britain.
3. Industry and education – Great Britain. 4.Vocational qualifications – Great
Britain. 5. Labor productivity – Great Britain. 6. Occupational training – Europe. 7.
Vocational education Europe. I. Title. II. Series: Occasional papers (National
Institute of Economic and Social Research): 48.
    HD5715.5.G7P7 1995
    331.25'92'0941–dc20   95–6517 CIP

ISBN 0 521 48305 0 hardback
ISBN 0 521 55667 8 paperback

To the memory of
PROFESSOR SIR RICHARD STONE
CBE FBA Nobel Laureate
1913–1991
an inspired and inspiring researcher in the social sciences

Founding Director of the Department of Applied Economics,
University of Cambridge, and a Governor of the National Institute of
Economic and Social Research

Contents

Tables

Preface

This slender volume is intended to provide policymakers, students and those interested in current affairs with a systematic introduction to the issues associated with the improvement of Britain's schooling and training systems. What are the best ways of raising educational and vocational standards to benefit from rapidly advancing technology, and to meet growing competition from developing countries? Modern economics textbooks tend to deal with these matters in simplified general terms, often referring simply to labour as a single homogeneous factor of production, and to its quality – if mentioned at all – in terms of average years of schooling of the workforce. For general theoretical or analytical purposes, that approach has a certain value. But anyone wishing to understand what should be done, and what can in practice be done, needs to enquire more deeply. These issues have become important in all advanced industrial countries – in the United States no less than in the United Kingdom – but while this book discusses underlying pressures and trends in general terms, when it comes to policy details the book naturally, because of its provenance, pays more attention to the needs of Britain.

Understanding what has succeeded in training and education in other countries is a valuable first step towards answering such policy questions. It is now nearly fifteen years since a small team at the National Institute began a series of empirical comparisons between Britain and adjacent Continental countries of productivity and workforce qualifications in matched samples of manufacturing plants in selected industries, together with associated comparisons at training colleges and schools. Results were published in a series of reports in the *National Institute Economic Review* as each set of comparisons was completed. The results considered as a whole are now here presented for the first time in a single book; the stimulus for doing so was provided by the Economic and Social Research Council who, in making their grant for the 1988–92 phase of work, suggested that the time had come to provide an overview. The present volume is the result. I have deliberately produced a short but systematic account, to help the busy general reader as well as the over-burdened student.

Researchers requiring details of the underlying studies will need to refer to the original reports. An initial selection of these studies was reproduced in a single compendium issued by NIESR in 1989; a second volume of subsequent studies will be made available by the National Institute shortly. References in the present book to articles reproduced in the compendia are shown in square brackets [ ], with full details at the end of the book; other references are given in full in the notes.

A briefer account of these studies, but one with a little more historical detail, was provided in my Keynes Lecture to the British Academy in October 1993 (subsequently published in the Proceedings of the Academy for that year). I am grateful to the Academy for allowing me to reproduce some sections of that lecture here.

The present volume and its underlying studies could not have been produced without the generous cooperation of very many people in industry and education – in Britain and on the Continent – who appreciated the value of comparative research in these areas, and who spoke to us frankly of current problems and trends. Equally, it could not have been produced without the help of a team of collaborators at the Institute; over the years that team has included Elaine Beadle, Helvia Bierhoff, Anne Daly, David Hitchens, Valerie Jarvis, Daniel T. Jones (now professor at the University of Cardiff), Hilary Steedman and Karin Wagner (now professor at the Technical University, Berlin). Fran Robinson saw the book through the press. I am indebted to them all for their cooperation.

In addition to the ESRC, I am happy to acknowledge financial support for a succession of related phases of this research programme by the Gatsby Charitable Foundation, the Leverhulme Trust and the Anglo-German Foundation for the Study of Industrial Society.

The publication of this volume coincides with my completion of around thirty years of research activities at the Institute under a succession of Governors and Directors. The financial organisation of research today requires the advance specification of projects, very often in some detail: it is only if that specification can in practice be treated elastically that original work is possible. I take this opportunity of expressing my thanks to the Institute and its supporters for its tolerance of – what must have seemed at times – my perhaps unduly idiosyncratic and elastic approach to my tasks.

I have dedicated this book to my late friend Richard Stone who, as my first employer, set my footsteps on the path of research.

S.J.P.
London
November 1994

1   General principles

The scope of this book

Education and training have appeared in the past decade as issues of great public and political concern in Britain; but the truth is that these issues were evident in Britain over a century ago, particularly to manufacturers close to international competition, as well as to certain more far-sighted economic observers – including the great Cambridge economist Alfred Marshall. In the past generation, not only Britain but almost all advanced industrialised countries have found it increasingly necessary to adjust to competition from newly industrialising countries. Policy debates on a great variety of reforms of schooling and training systems are now widespread; and both in industrialised and in newly industrialising countries the need for higher levels of education and for modern work-training are seen as almost self-evident priorities.

    It is the aim of this book to present a brief systematic introduction to these issues. The account given here draws heavily on a series of empirical international comparisons – carried out by the National Institute – of productivity, schooling and training in which Britain has been compared with France, Germany, the Netherlands, Switzerland and Japan as examples of rapidly advancing industrial countries. Matched samples of manufacturing plants formed the foundations of our comparisons between Britain and Germany and provide much of the empirical detail reported here.

    The following familiar questions illustrate in more detail the concerns that have motivated this book: have advances associated with automation been so very different from technical changes in previous generations that virtually new problems have arisen in relation to training, retraining and schooling requirements? How are skill shortages related to wage levels? What do we mean by a 'skill shortage': is it like a scarcity of gold, which in reality is always available in the market if we are prepared to pay for it; or is it like butter in war time, the controlled price of which is too low for suppliers to come forward? Why can we not rely on the market mechanism to supply the 'right' amounts of schooling and of training that are required – whether from a narrow private economic point of view, or from a wider social perspective? Is it more important to subsidise training in job-specific skills, or to subsidise training in general skills?

Many previous statistical investigations have been concerned with the 'returns to education'; they have asked whether an extra year of schooling, or university attendance, has subsequently yielded a higher income commensurate with the sacrifice of forgone earnings made by the pupil, and other costs borne by parents and by taxpayers. We need to emphasise at the outset that statistical investigations of that kind have been based on the earnings of samples of individuals *within a given country* – they ask, for example, what are the consequences for an average English 16-year-old's earnings of an extra year's schooling of the kind given in England to youngsters of that age. They do not look for the consequences of giving the very different kind of schooling and training available in, say, France or Germany. It is the latter more difficult and more important question that concerns us here. To understand how countries differ, and what policies are appropriate for Britain today, we shall have to ask not simply how many years are spent by a pupil in school or in training, but rather what is the subject-matter that has been taught and learnt, and what proportions of pupils reach various levels of competence.

If anything can be said here at manageable length on a subject as vast as education and training, it is only because this book takes primarily an economic point of view; that is to say, we are concerned with the long-term effects of education and training on the Wealth of Nations, including the consequences for unemployment among the young and unskilled. Because our focus is primarily on economic aspects, it is necessary to say clearly at the outset what should perhaps be taken as obvious – that education has much wider objectives than merely preparing citizens to become more efficient 'cogs in the industrial–economic machine';[1] the history of the horrors of the twentieth century and its totalitarian states should be sufficient warning against that narrow view of the purposes of education.

Finding the right balance of school-time to be devoted to matters connected with work, compared with time devoted to general (academic) studies, has everywhere become a more important issue as compulsory full-time schooling ages have been raised in the past century step by step beyond the age of puberty – in Britain, from the age of ten in 1876, to twelve by the end of the century, to fourteen after the First World War, to fifteen shortly after the Second World War, and to sixteen in 1973. In some American states full-time education is compulsory till eighteen; in the Netherlands and Germany some form of part-time education is compulsory till seventeen and eighteen respectively. It seems that after the age of about fourteen a proportion of pupils in all countries – but different proportions according to the schooling system and social background – become dissatisfied with what they see as the study of subjects not 'relevant' (a modern keyword) to their current lives or subsequent careers. Some become frustrated and rebel; when they subsequently seek employment at sixteen they may know less, and are less suited to further learning, than if they had left school earlier and spent the intervening years as an apprentice following a systematic course of training for a skilled career, or employed initially on simple tasks, and progressing on the basis of experience and opportunities to more complex tasks.

Detailed practical matters on the way specimen branches of industry operate in other countries in comparison with Britain, and how schooling and training are organised, will occupy us in most of this book. The remainder of this first chapter sets out some general, but not always obvious, principles to help in understanding why these issues have recently acquired greater seriousness; and why they are not easily to be solved either by relying on market forces, nor simply by the taxpayer providing more funding for education without worrying on what those funds are to be spent.

Technology and the demand for skills

Let us begin by distinguishing in a schematic way two phases in the progress of technology: the earlier phase of *mechanisation* – predominant, say, till the 1960s – and the subsequent and continuing phase of *automation*. Both are familiar aspects of the progressive application of human knowledge to industry, leading to higher productivity and higher living standards. For the engineer, automation is often seen as just a further step in the development of mechanisation. But for the economist and social scientist there is an important difference in the way that these two phases in the progress of technology affect the demand for skills and the market for employment; the distinction is often expressed by asking whether technical progress involves a de-skilling of the workforce, or requires increased skills.

The predominant feature of the phase of *mechanisation* was the replacement of skilled craftsmen by machines operated by unskilled or semi-skilled operators: instead of a craftsman sawing and carefully filing a piece of metal to size using basic hand-tools, an unskilled operator – pushing the pedal of a mechanised power-press – was able to achieve consistently satisfactory results in a fraction of the time. In that phase of technological progress the demand for unskilled workers increased step by step as the use of machinery was extended in one application after another. Skilled craftsmen were displaced by machinery; but they were usually able to make use of their superior knowledge and experience by filling the increased demand for tool-setters, supervisors or chargehands of the unskilled. If that possibility was not open, they worked as 'setter-operators' or, if all else failed, as operators. Problems of re-employment as a result of mechanisation thus affected mainly the intermediate stratum of craftsmen, and were not insoluble.

The predominant feature of the current phase of *automation* is that the work of far greater numbers of unskilled operators of machines is being replaced by automatic devices, for example, for feeding, activating, unloading the workpiece, or transferring it to the next machine. Those displaced unskilled operators do not, however, have any natural alternative employment since they are not qualified to fill the increased demand for technicians, supervisors and maintenance engineers needed to service such automated machinery.

The advance of automation has affected office work of many sorts (for example, in banking and insurance) as well as the type of direct production just mentioned. Automated production lines often involve expensive machinery, which only a foolish employer would risk damaging by allowing an inexperienced trainee to work or supervise. The result has been a fall in demand for technically unqualified personnel, and especially inexperienced youngsters; this fall in demand must be expected to continue as automation is increasingly applied in one process after another.[2]

For the sake of clarity it is perhaps necessary to emphasise that there has been a *reversal* in the demand for unskilled workers as technology has advanced. Whereas the demand for unskilled workers increased during the earlier phase of mechanisation – and that demand was obviously easy to meet – we are now in a phase where the demand for unskilled workers is decreasing. The ensuing problems are very difficult.

Consider, first, the change in skill-differentials. During the earlier phase of mechanisation, the wages of the unskilled rose, not only in real terms and with the general rise in productivity, but relatively to the wages of craftsmen for whom demand had not increased as rapidly. The narrowing of skill differentials, and the reduction in the inequality of earnings, was seen by many as socially beneficial (though some worried that it might go too far and reduce incentives for the acquisition of higher skills). But with the arrival of automation the level of wages that can be offered by employers to unskilled employees, being governed by their potential marginal productivity in a world of new technology, falls relative to those who are technically skilled. It may fall below the level regarded as conventionally acceptable, as embodied in the level of social security benefits. More or less severe unemployment of the unskilled is the inevitable result.[3]

Second, during the phase of mechanisation, schooling aspirations and standards were affected by the increased demand for unskilled labour, and interacted with other educational ideals. Technical qualifications were seen as essential for a narrow stratum of youngsters; but for the great majority of youngsters the strengthened plea of 'progressive' educationists was to allow a child to grow up naturally (following Rousseau), without the 'tyranny of exams', and for only minimal vocational preparation during the years of compulsory schooling.

What the majority needed for their jobs could be learnt rapidly enough in due course in the first few days (or hours) at their job. Schooling institutions, and habits of the existing stock of teachers, change only slowly in response to the changing technological demands of the economy and in response to the evolving ideas of leading educational theorists. While these tendencies have affected all countries, they have done so at different rates of development; each country thus provided different mixes of schooling and training opportunities for youngsters when automation arrived and, almost overnight, began reducing the demand for unskilled and technically unqualified labour.

Later chapters will detail the consequences of the different mixes of educational ideals and institutions in Britain and other countries. At this stage we need perhaps only emphasise the reversals in educational tidal waves: the need for more widespread general and technical schooling in the very early phases of mechanisation in the nineteenth and earlier part of the twentieth century, followed by a shift in emphasis in Britain towards general – and away from technical – schooling in the middle of the twentieth century, now followed by a hesitant return to a greater vocational and technical bias in the curriculum at secondary schools. Two dates in recent British educational history – a quarter of a century apart – illustrate concretely these changing tendencies in schooling; the first is 1955 when what was thought to be the last technical secondary school for 11–16-year-olds in England was abolished under the signature of a (Conservative) Minister of Education, and the second is 1988 when an initiative for City Technology Colleges for the same age-groups was launched by the government (again Conservative).

The market for skills

We have so far spoken broadly of skilled and unskilled sections of the workforce, taking it for granted that these will be understood as shorthand for a real world in which there is a spectrum of partially substitutable skills. It is convenient for exposition to continue with that simplification while we consider the consequences of the inevitable time lags in the supply of skills, and of other difficulties standing in the way of smooth market adjustments; these difficulties have made social intervention necessary in virtually all countries to ensure adequate education and training in order to benefit more rapidly from advances in technology.

In periods of unchanging technology of the kind Adam Smith must have envisaged when explaining wage differentials between 'blacksmiths, fishermen, tailors and carpenters', it was sufficient to point to the 'difficulty and expense of learning' different occupations, their 'agreeableness or disagreeableness' and similar factors. Such differences in 'the whole of the advantages and disadvantages' of different occupations led to well-recognised and stable differentials in rewards; they provided appropriate incentives for a continuing sufficiency of persons to enter each trade, and equilibrated demand and supply in the market for skills. The main worries were whether 'at the age at which young people choose their professions' there is a 'presumptuous hope of success' which leads to over-ambitious decisions; and whether (as later writers such as Pigou emphasised) the short-sighted tendency of young persons led them unduly to choose immediate income from unskilled work in preference to the delayed advantages resulting from longer preparation for a career.[4]

The difficulties of making a rational choice of career on the basis of current wage differentials are obviously much greater when technology changes rapidly. Let us follow patiently the sequence of steps after an unexpected rise in demand for a particular skill as a result of technical progress, or as a result of a rise in home or foreign demand for products using that skill. At existing wages employers require more people with that skill than have so far been forthcoming; would that shortage disappear if wage differentials for that skill were raised?

The longer the period required for training, the longer it will take for additional supplies of trained personnel to come forward, and the more likely it is that initially unduly high and confusing wage signals will go out to youngsters. As John Hicks put it: 'The level of wages which is needed to attract labour quickly into an expanding trade is, however, higher than that which is required to maintain the larger labour force; but, having once risen, the differential does not fall back easily. It is therefore highly probable that actual wage systems are full of differentials that have lost their economic function.'[5] Oscillations in wage rates are more likely in occupations with long periods of training and where substitutable skills are few, so that the short-term elasticity of supply is low; 'professional' occupations, characterised by lengthy training and restrictions on the entry of those without formal qualifications (for example, lawyers in most countries), have shown considerable year-to-year variations in initial salaries, with traces of a cycle related to length of training.[6]

Fortunately, the reality of most occupations is not quite so confusing. When arranging a wage with a potential employee, an employer who values his reputation as a 'good employer' looks forward as much as the employee to the maintenance of that wage in the future, and to gradual increases in the light of experience and general progress. A subsequent reduction in wage rates is usually unthinkable. If an unexpected shortage of a particular skill arises, some smaller employers may immediately raise wages to ensure that they do not go short of that skill; and some adventurous employees become 'self-employed' and hire out their services at high rates on short-term contracts. But large employers, and most employees who like working in a stable environment, try to agree on wages within a long-term framework: temporary shortages are expected to be met by working overtime, sometimes supported by 'no doubt relatively disorderly bonuses above the agreed minima', and by delivery delays; while surpluses of a particular skill are dealt with by short-time working, redeployment and gradual retirement – rather than by discharging labour and a radical adjustment of wage rates.[7] In sectors of the economy dominated by this approach (for example, large firms in unionised sectors of the UK) wage fluctuations will obviously be dampened as compared with a 'hire-and-fire' economy with short-term wage contracts.

The problem of providing adequate wage signals to youngsters deciding on which trade to enter and how much training to undertake is compounded by trade-union notions of 'customary differentials' and 'established relativities'. These prevent an employer offering higher wages for one grade of skill without soon having to meet unions' demands for corresponding rises in other grades for which there may be no shortage.[8]

In relation to occupations requiring long periods of training, employers also sometimes argue that there is no point in raising wages since it merely redistributes the existing stock of skills, when what they want is an increased stock – to be supplied, for example, as a result of more places for engineering students at colleges (financed by the government). That argument overlooks the short-term beneficial consequences of higher wages on the use of the existing stock; higher wages will lead to (a) a redistribution away from less urgent to more urgent uses of those skills, (b) a more intensive use of those scarce skills by the provision of support staff trained to lower levels, and (c) the provision of better equipment to permit more intensive employment of those scarce skills. Such substitution might be expensive in the long term, but helps to bridge the gap in the short term; unless wages are raised in the short term, the incentive to economise in scarce skills in these ways is neither as great nor as pervasive.

The markets for labour skills are thus complex, even if they were free to operate without constraints imposed by social ideals, government legislation and trade-union pressures. In the postwar period in Britain, general egalitarian ideals were expressed in increased social security benefits and more widespread minimum-wage agreements. It is thus not surprising to find that skill differentials were compressed, and that inadequate signals went to school-leavers having to decide on their occupations and on how much training was justified.

Who pays for training?

Training is expensive – in terms of production and wages forgone by the trainee and fees for college attendance. How much of those total costs should be borne by the employer, how much by the trainee, and how much by the government? And what traps must be avoided by a government which decides to intervene to increase national levels of training? These are complex issues on which there has often been much misunderstanding: it will be helpful to begin, following the analysis by Becker, by distinguishing – if only conceptually – training for general (or transferable) skills from training for specific skills required only in a particular job.[9] We shall first consider how the market for the two types of skill would operate under competitive conditions, and then consider the consequences of market imperfections and the likely effects of interventions.

General skills might be thought of as those possessed, for example, by a qualified secretary in a large commercial city, or by a qualified electrician who can work for a number of employers in a large industrial area; on the other hand, specific skills are those required in a particular job with a particular employer, say, making locks for suitcases in a region where there is only a single factory making such locks. It might seem that the important difference lies in the nature of the skills, the former benefiting from longer studies at college and the passing of public examinations, and the latter being essentially acquired by learning 'on the job' at that employer; we shall see, however, that a more important difference lies in the nature of the local labour market – that is, whether there are sufficient alternative employers in the region who are prepared to offer employment making use of those skills.

In the case of general skills, the rewards for acquiring them accrue to the employee in the form of higher wages, as determined by the market, reflecting both the higher value of a skilled employee's contribution to production and the costs of training. If an employer – rather than the employee – invests in training in general skills, he runs the risk that the employee, after qualifying as a skilled person, will leave for another employer whose policy is not to incur such expenditures – and who is consequently in a better position to offer higher wages. This is often known as the problem of 'poaching', or the problem of the 'free rider'; any implied moral condemnation must be ignored here while we seek an objective understanding of the economic pressures that are operative. The point to be emphasised is that under competitive conditions, and in the absence of government subsidies for training, an employer can provide training for general skills only if the employee is prepared to accept substantially lower wages during the period of training (an important feature of Continental training systems). In other words, if training in general skills is carried out in a competitive labour market, it is the trainee who has to bear the costs, and who in due course reaps the rewards of higher differential pay. By balancing the costs of earnings forgone and of tuition during the period of training against the discounted value of higher earnings during subsequent working years, a potential trainee decides whether training for that skill is worthwhile, or whether he or she should choose some other skilled occupation, or perhaps choose to remain unskilled.

On the other hand, specific skills – in the way they have been defined here to explain the conceptual point at issue – are of value only in a particular employment. Having acquired them with one employer, a trainee is in no better position to obtain a higher-paid job with another employer than previously. If training in such skills is to be undertaken, it has thus to be financed by the employer rather than by the employee. After training, the employee's wages need not rise, since there is no alternative demand for such skills; the improved productivity resulting from training accrues to the employer rather than to the employee. Correspondingly, it is the employer (rather than the employee) who has to engage in balancing the cost of training against the discounted value of the trainee's expected higher productivity in deciding how much training is worthwhile.

That is, however, too simple an account of how the market for specific skills works, for the following reason. The lower the rate of expected labour turnover, the more worthwhile will specific training be to the employer, and the amount of specific training employers are prepared to finance will increase, in respect of both the number of trainees and the amount invested in each. To avoid capricious changes of jobs, and the loss of investment in specific training, the employer thus has an incentive to offer the trainee some share in his increased productivity; this may take the form of bonuses based on individual achievements or wage-rises according to length of service (the latter is given much emphasis in the Japanese system with its venerated ideal of 'life-long employment'). Such rises in wages in response to the acquisition of *specific* skills differ from those accruing to persons who have acquired *general* skills in that the former embody only a fraction of the value of the improved productivity sufficient to prevent them moving to another employer, rather than the market value of the whole of that improvement. The remainder of the value of that improvement is necessary to compensate the employer for the costs incurred in training the employee in those specific skills.

The size of the fraction of higher productivity accruing to the employee from specific training may be quite small if opportunities for changes in employment are negligible; but that fraction could grow, as theorists have pointed out, if circumstances permit a long-term agreement for employment and accelerated training.[10] This would require the trainee to accept lower wages initially than could be obtained elsewhere, and so bear part of the cost of accelerated training (including a smaller contribution to output during that shorter training period) in order to become more productive at an earlier date, and reap a share in that higher productivity at an earlier date. Such an arrangement requires trust on both sides and is difficult to enforce (suppose the trainee does not live up to expectations, is the employer still under an obligation to raise wages?); it is closer to apprenticeship arrangements of earlier times – involving an introduction to the mysteries of the employer's trade which the apprentice was obliged not to reveal to others – than to modern conditions in which commitments on future services cannot be taken as having effective binding force in practice – irrespective of the legal situation (the costs of going to law are too great in relation to any benefits). Analogous conditions are, however, today found in large, highly specialised firms where those joining the firm do so with a long-term career with that firm in mind.

Insofar as employers bear the costs of any training, it is in their interests to channel such training as far as possible towards *specific* skills needed in their own establishments, and to avoid providing training which – if the trained employee subsequently leaves – might benefit a competitor. On the other hand, the trainee's interests lie in the acquisition of general skills which have a recognised marketable value, and which will provide a degree of security in case he or she needs to change employers.

Theoretical evaluation of a market for skills

It may help in understanding the complexity of the factors leading to skill-shortages if we consider for a moment, and entirely hypothetically, the course of the 'natural economic evolution' of the labour market. We start from an imaginary early stage – not necessarily feudal — in which transport facilities were limited and there was a single predominant local employer (Stage A); next, we consider conditions where there are better transport facilities and each employee can effectively choose among a few employers (Stage B); finally, we suppose that the economy has developed sufficiently so that an employee can choose among very many employers (Stage C).

In Stage A there is only a single employer and all skills are effectively 'specific' skills; that single employer, in accordance with the argument above, provides and finances all the training that is economically justifiable; if a shortage of a particular skill emerges for any reason – new technology, inadequate planning – it is that employer's responsibility to put it right.

As the economy develops and the number of employers increases, some of the skills required in production will be the same for a number of employers (Stage B); these correspond to the 'general' skills discussed above. We may suppose that there are sufficiently few local employers so that they can agree, formally or informally, not to poach each other's trained employees; they may also agree to provide common training facilities in those general skills; and they are likely to adopt devices to discourage change of employment, such as loss of pension rights on leaving, or paying seniority allowances in proportion to length of tenure with the *current* employer. The responsibility for adequate training at this stage continues to remain with each employer, perhaps aided by the likelihood that the general skills required are low in proportion to specific skills gained simultaneously in the course of work. This situation corresponds in many ways to recent, and even current, actuality in small towns with dominant specialist employers.

As the number of employers increases in large towns, Stage C is reached where there is a greater demand for common general skills, and employers are prepared to employ anyone who comes to the door offering the requisite skills. Employers continue to provide training in the additional specific skills required for their own production in addition to general skills, but they gradually give up training in those important general skills that they all require – since it is not in the interests of any individual employer to finance them. If wage differentials emerge that are sufficient to induce potential employees to finance their own general training, all may be well; but if differentials are inadequate – and, as we have seen, there are many reasons why this may occur – then shortages of general skills are the likely consequence. Some form of social intervention is then required to remedy the deficiencies in general skills.

Remedies for inadequate training

We are now ready to consider possible remedies for obstacles standing in the way of adequate training in general skills. The first obstacle, as explained in previous pages, may be that skill differentials may be too compressed and not adequately responsive to changing technological requirements. Second, young trainees' typically limited capital resources, combined with the short-sightedness of youth and the urgency of immediate needs, may lead them to discount too heavily the benefits of a higher income at later dates; with inadequate parental support, or because of a desire for early independence, too many young persons therefore choose work requiring little or no training. Governmental subsidies offered to employers and educational institutions, and subsidised loans to trainees, are ways of offsetting these factors. Another possible remedy is to make a period of vocational training compulsory, in the same way that general full-time schooling is compulsory up to a certain age (this has been one of the buttresses of Continental systems). Third, improving the reliability and objectivity of vocational qualifications helps to improve information and the workings of the market for skills; the better the information conveyed by a qualification, the greater is the demand by employers for recognised skills, and the greater are the incentives for youngsters to acquire such qualifications. In the absence of reliable market signals on shortages of general skills conveyed via wage differentials, it becomes a matter of judgement (rather than precise calculation) as to when such remedies have yielded adequate increases in skilled personnel in total; and it also becomes a matter of judgement whether the distribution of training among the various occupations is sufficiently close to what is required for maximum economic efficiency.

The main obstacle to adequate training in specific skills is very different – it is that of excessive labour turnover. Subsidies would encourage more training but, if labour turnover remained high, the additional training would disappear down the same drain. The balance struck by employers in comparing returns from specific training with its costs – bearing in mind the likely rate of labour turnover – is not obviously wrong; a government subsidy for training in specific skills is not therefore a good use of tax-payers' money.

It would be better to focus on what needs to be done to reduce labour turnover – not simply in terms of more friendly faces in the personnel department and the like (as industrial psychologists and management consultants are happy to recommend), but in terms of adequate economic incentives. A certain degree of labour turnover is desirable since occasional mistaken decisions by either side are inevitable, especially at young ages; but labour turnover becomes excessive if an employee feels constricted by the rewards for experience and skills offered by the present employer, and concludes that the only way to advance is by changing employers. Arrangements to pay the same wage for all young employees of a given age, with rises on their birthdays ('wage for age' agreements), are wide-spread among large organisations. They have the charms of appearing equitable – a prime consideration with trade unions – and of being administratively convenient – a prime consideration for wage administrators in large firms; but such agreements usually do not do enough to encourage those employees who have mastered the requisite skills to stay on, nor do they provide encouragement for a more rapid mastery of those skills.

In reality almost all training consists of a mix of general and specific skills: but the point of this distinction becomes particularly clear when we consider the effects of government intervention to increase training by means of subsidies to employers. As explained, employers are always tempted to make training as specific to their own firms' needs as possible whereas the important shortages which subsidies should attempt to remedy are of general skills. It is therefore essential to marry any scheme for subsidised training with a scheme for the control of the content of training, to ensure that it is sufficiently broad and general.

This chapter has attempted no more than to set the framework of discussion for the remainder of the book: to outline the broad technological issues and economic principles, and so provide a framework for understanding the different ways that governments in different countries have intervened in education and training to improve industrial performance. In the next chapter we shall compare the proportions of the working population in different countries reaching specified levels of vocational skills, and the institutional arrangements that go with them – the colleges, their links with industrial experience, and the breadth and depth of qualification levels. The relation between better training and better industrial performance is the subject of our third chapter; and the role of schooling foundations for subsequent training is examined in chapter four. The final chapter discusses the prospects and long-standing difficulties of putting into practice in Britain the kind of improvements in schooling and training that seem desirable in the light of the comparisons and investigations set out in this book.

2 Preparation for work in Britain and elsewhere

This chapter describes what happens in practice in Britain and other countries in relation to vocational training and the award of qualifications in general vocational skills. We shall begin with the German example: Germany's long-established and detailed training system, its industrial success, and its similarity to Britain in size and resources, make that country of special interest. We then describe more briefly what happens in some other countries – France, the Netherlands, Switzerland and Japan.[1]

At the outset it needs to be noted that training varies *within* all countries in standards and content, and it has never been easy to arrive at a summary view of average differences *between* countries. Earlier investigations – which go back at least to the Royal Commission on Technical Instruction of a century ago (the 'Samuelson Commission' of 1882–4) – relied on visits to selected firms and technical colleges to form broad impressions of differences between countries as a whole in average levels of training. More recent international comparisons have often been confined to those qualifying with university degrees, that is, such studies looked only at the tip of the iceberg. It is only in the past twenty years or so, with the availability of statistical surveys of the labour force as a whole – carried out with some degree of international coordination of sampling practices and questionnaires – that broader international comparisons of educational and vocational qualifications of the whole spectrum of the workforce have become possible, and have also become more reliable. It has now become entirely clear that inter-country differences in the proportions of the workforce trained to various levels of vocational competence are very substantial indeed; we thus also need to examine in this chapter the main features of the institutional arrangements that have brought about those differences.

Magnitude of international differences in intermediate vocational qualifications

A summary view of workforce qualifications in Britain and Germany at the end of the 1980s, and a decade earlier — towards the end of the 1970s — is set out in table 2.1 on the basis of information gathered by official sample surveys of households. In this table the workforce is divided into three broad qualification-groups: those with university degrees or equivalent (such as membership of engineering institutes in Britain); those with intermediate qualifications of a vocational sort, such as City and Guilds craft certificates; and those without vocational qualifications. Some in this last group may have general educational qualifications such as, in Britain, a General Certificate of Secondary Education (GCSE) in one or more subjects; or, in Germany, a satisfactory leaving certificate from the equivalent of our Secondary Modern schools (*Hauptschulabschluss*). We shall comment further on the definitions of these vocational groups in a moment; but the following clearly important conclusions should be stated at once.

First, there is now negligible difference between the countries in the proportion of the workforce holding university degrees. They now account for about 10 per cent of the workforce in both countries, and have increased equally rapidly in both countries from some 6–7 per cent a decade ago.

Second, the overriding difference between the countries lies at the intermediate level of qualification: Germany has just over 60 per cent with such qualifications, compared with a little under 30 per cent in Britain. A small decline in Britain is shown for the past decade in this category, from 30 to 27 per cent;[2] the numbers entering apprenticeship in Britain have fallen drastically in this period, and a genuine fall in the stock of qualified persons at this level is not entirely implausible. Nevertheless, the apparent fall is perhaps small enough to be attributed to imperfections in the underlying sample surveys, or in the approximations adopted to ensure definitional comparability between the countries. Perhaps the more important conclusion to be drawn is that, despite many initiatives in Britain in this period to increase vocational training, the proportion of the workforce with vocational qualifications at this level has not risen. The modest rise in the German proportion at this level is probably a genuine reflection of the rising proportion of school-leavers completing an apprenticeship. Apprentices in Germany now include school-leavers not only from *Hauptschulen* (the equivalent of our Secondary Modern schools) and *Realschulen* (Middle schools), but also increasing proportions from their *Gymnasien* (Grammar schools); one in twelve vocational trainees had attained a Grammar school leaving qualification (*Abitur*) in 1983, rising to one in seven in 1989.[3]

Table 2.1 *Summary comparisons of workforce qualifications in Britain, 1976 and 1988, and West Germany, 1978 and 1987*

	Britain		Germany	
	1976(a)	1988	1978	1987
All activities				
University qualifications(b)	6	10	7	10
Intermediate vocational qualifications(c)	30	27	60	64
No vocational qualifications(d)	64	63	33	26
	100	100	100	100
All manufacturing				
University qualifications(b)	3	7	3	6
Intermediate vocational qualifications(c)	29	31	61	64
No vocational qualifications(d)	68	62	36	29
	100	100	100	100
All non-manufacturing				
University qualifications(b)	7	11	9	12
Intermediate vocational qualifications(c)	31	26	59	63
No vocational qualifications(d)	63	63	32	25
	100	100	100	100

Sources: Britain: General Household Surveys, 1974–8, Labour Force Survey, 1988. Germany: *Microzensus* 1978 and 1987.
Notes:
(a) Average of surveys for 1974–8.
(b) For Britain, members of professional institutions with qualifications of degree standard, and graduate teachers; for Germany, includes graduates of technical institutes (*Fachhochschulen*) and engineering colleges (*Ingenieurschulen*).
(c) Craft and technician qualifications, including (for Britain) non-examined time-served apprenticeships.
(d) Includes some with general educational qualifications but no vocational qualifications.

Third, it follows that nearly two-thirds of the British workforce are vocationally unqualified – in contrast with only a quarter in Germany at the end of the 1980s. Put another way, we may say that the typical (or modal) member of the workforce in Germany has attained a vocational qualification at craft level or above, while the typical member of the workforce in Britain is vocationally unqualified.

Speaking very broadly, these sample surveys of the labour force give numerical expression to what has long been made familiar by industrially concerned observers as well as by novelists describing German society – namely, the greater 'middle-class' weight of German society and associated preoccupation with qualification levels. This contrasts with Britain's heavier 'popularist' social centre of gravity and the associated greater pressures towards 'popular' norms. Support may also be found in these figures for the view that Britain has been more sharply a country of 'two nations' than Germany: those who have attained qualifications in Britain contrast more strongly with the unqualified majority, while German society has been buffered by a broader intermediate stratum.

The disparities between the proportions in the top and bottom qualification classes have narrowed in both countries in the past decade, as suggested by table 2.1. But there is a difference between the countries. The narrowing that has taken place in Britain is attributable more to an increase of those with higher educational qualifications than to a decline of those without vocational qualifications; the Germans have managed to do both. This is not to deny that Britain has seen a decline in this period in those without educational qualifications; but that change has been due to an increase in *general schooling* qualifications (such as GCSE) rather than to any increase in those who hold *vocational* qualifications.

Intermediate qualifications can be divided into two categories – technicians and craftsmen, as they are often termed in industry; the former usually involve longer full-time instruction at technical colleges, while the latter are more often based on part-time instruction. Of the 64 per cent of the total German workforce with intermediate qualifications in 1987, some 7 per cent were in the technician category and 57 per cent in the craftsman category; in Britain, of the 27 per cent of the total workforce with intermediate qualifications, some 7 per cent were in the technician category – the same proportion as in Germany – and 20 per cent were in the craftsman category. Thus, there is negligible difference between these countries at the technician (or 'upper intermediate') level, just as there is negligible difference between the countries at the university-degree level: the difference lies virtually entirely at the craftsman, or 'lower intermediate' level.

Let us next consider separately the manufacturing and non-manufacturing sectors of the economy (see the lower part of table 2.1). University graduates in both countries are to be found more frequently in non-manufacturing sectors of the economy, particularly in the professions – law, medicine, education – and in government administration. In manufacturing industry as a whole, university graduates are to be found only about half as frequently as in the non-manufacturing sectors of both economies (6–7 per cent compared to 11–12 per cent). There are, however, certain manufacturing industries which are knowledge-intensive and depend very much on university graduates – such as chemicals, petroleum refining, electrical and instrument engineering; in these industries graduates form up to 14 per cent of the workforce.

More detail is shown in table 2.2, which divides the economy into ten manufacturing industries and a dozen non-manufacturing sectors. It is noteworthy that Britain now employs a slightly greater proportion of graduates in many manufacturing industries than Germany;[4] but that gap in favour of Britain is small – at the most 5 per cent of the workforce – compared with the 35 per cent gap in favour of Germany at the intermediate level of vocational qualification. Germany's advantage at the intermediate level extends remarkably throughout the whole range of manufacturing and non-manufacturing sectors listed in this table, varying from a minimum additional 25 per cent of the workforce with vocational qualifications in engineering, to an additional 50 per cent in textile and related industries and in financial services (insurance, banking, and so on).

University degrees: too few engineers

We may now look more closely at the growth and main subject-specialisations of the qualifications awarded in the two countries. Let us begin with university degrees: much the same total number of first degrees (about 120,000) were awarded in the two countries in 1986–7 by universities and other institutes of higher education (including polytechnics and the Open University in Britain, and including *Fachhochschulen* – technical universities – in Germany). In both countries there has been a remarkable doubling in the total numbers graduating in the previous decade (from some 70,000 in 1976); and those rates of expression and those similarities have continued in more recent years for which figures have since become available.[5] These comparisons with Germany thus provide no support for any contention that Britain is out of step in the total number or rate of growth of its university graduates.

But very large differences persist in the subject-areas studied, with students in Germany choosing more vocationally oriented courses than in Britain. For example, within that same total of first degrees, Germany produced 60 per cent more engineering and technology graduates than Britain (26,000 compared with 16,000) while, conversely, Britain produced

Table 2.2 *Vocational qualifications of the workforce by industrial group in Great Britain, 1988, and West Germany, 1987*

| Industrial group(a) | Employ-ment in each industry as % of total workforce | | Persons with stated quali-fication levels as % of work-force in each industrial group | | | | | |
			Univers-ity (b)		Inter-mediate (c)		None (d)	
Manufacturing industries	B	G	B	G	B	G	B	G
Metal manufacture	2.2	3.9	4	3	34	64	62	33
Chemicals & artificial fibres	1.4	3.6	14	9	26	62	60	29
Petroleum products	0.2	0.1	13	12	39	65	48	23
Engineering: mechanical	2.7	5.4	7	7	43	69	50	24
Engineering: electrical & instrument	3.7	4.8	13	12	31	62	56	27
Vehicles, transport equpt.	2.8	3.3	7	7	41	66	52	27
Food, drink & tobacco	2.3	3.0	5	2	21	65	74	33
Textiles, leather & footwear	2.4	2.3	3	1	16	60	81	39
Paper & printing	2.2	1.6	9	4	30	67	61	29
Other manufacturing	3.6	3.2	4	3	28	66	68	31

Sources: Britain: Based on OPCS, *Labour Force Survey, 1988,* unpublished tabulations; the figures shown here depend in part on estimates (see Appendix A therein). Germany: *Microzensus,* 1987, unpublished tabulation.

Notes:

(a) Based on British Standard Industrial Classification (revised 1980); the German industrial groups have been matched as closely as possible from a classification based on 165 sub-groups. The matching of the final three groups (services and public administration) is not wholly satisfactory; it seems possible that the German sample has classified under 'public administration' some (for example, education or health administrators) who in Britain are classified under 'professional and scientific services'.

(b) For Britain, includes members of professional institutions with qualifications of degree standard (Census of Population 'b' level), and graduate teachers. For Germany, includes graduates of technical institutes (*Fachhochschulen*) and engineering colleges (*Ingenieurschulen*).

(c) Includes non-graduate qualifications, including apprenticeships (in Britain also time-served and non-examined apprenticeships).

(d) For Britain, half of this group consists of those reporting no educational or vocational qualification; the other half consists of those with educational

Table 2.2 *continued*

Industrial group(a)	Employ-ment in each industry as % of total workforce		Persons with stated quali-fication levels as % of work-force in each industrial group					
			Univers-ity (b)		Inter-mediate (c)		None (d)	
Non-manufacturing	B	G	B	G	B	G	B	G
Agriculture, forestry & fishing	2.2	4.4	4	2	20	46	76	52
Mining & quarrying	0.9	1.1	10	6	34	64	56	30
Gas, electricity & water	1.4	1.0	13	8	39	76	48	16
Construction	7.6	6.5	5	4	43	71	52	25
Transport & communications	6.2	6.2	6	6	27	73	67	21
Distributive trades	15.3	12.4	4	4	18	73	78	23
Hotels & catering	4.2	2.5	3	2	20	56	77	42
Insurance, banking & finance	3.7	3.4	12	8	12	77	76	15
Business services (& leasing)	6.6	4.1	24.	22	18	60	58	18
Education, health & scientific services	12.3	9.9	24	37	34	46	42	17
Miscellaneous services	9.7	7.1	8	10	26	57	66	33
Public administration & defence	6.3	10.0	14	15	24	66	62	19

(Notes *continued*)
qualifications (e.g. O–level, A–level, CSE) but without vocational qualification. For Germany, this group consists mainly of those who have not taken, or have failed, the *Berufsschule* final examination; the great majority have some form of general school-leaving qualification.

twice as many graduates in pure sciences as Germany (27,000 compared with 13,000).[6] Of equal interest, Germany produced more graduates in business administration and related social studies (46,000 compared with 30,000), while Britain produced more graduates in languages and arts (30,000 compared with 12,000).[7] It is these differences in *subject-speciali-sation* at university – rather than in total number of degrees awarded – that must be expected to affect differences between the countries in the techni-cal and organisational efficiency of their industries.

These comparisons touch on a number of difficult policy questions on the government financing of students at British universities according to their subject of study. Rather than being in favour of a further blanket expansion of universities, we need to ask, for example, whether the number of university places available in languages and arts should in some way be restricted; or, within the same total resources, whether the length of course might be reduced for some students of these subjects to two years (leading to an Associate Degree, as in the United States). In engineering, on the other hand, it needs to be emphasised that German first-degree courses are longer than in Britain, extending to six years, and are more practically oriented; their object is to produce a graduate ready to assume the full responsibilities of employment, where the British engineering graduate requires several years of subsequent practical experience before qualifying as a full Chartered Engineer. The current tendency to extend the typical British three-year engineering course to four years brings Britain closer to Continental practice.[8] This is not the place to argue these questions fully; it is necessary here only to be clear that a blanket expansion of university places should not be taken as being obviously desirable in itself.

Vocational qualifications: their breadth and depth

As we have seen, it is at the level of intermediate vocational qualifications that the gap between Britain and Germany is largest. We next describe the institutional processes which lead so many more young persons in Germany to undertake vocational training, and then compare the standards attained in the two countries.

After completing compulsory full-time schooling, generally at the age of fifteen (that is, generally a year younger than in Britain), virtually all pupils in Germany who are not otherwise continuing in full-time education attend a part-time vocational college for the equivalent of one day a week for three years, that is, usually to the age of eighteen. There are a number of exceptions and variations to that pattern, but they need not detain us at this stage: it is important only to appreciate that close to two-thirds of all young persons aged sixteen to nineteen in Germany are now enrolled in such part-time vocational colleges on courses associated with their status as a trainee or apprentice. A substantial period of vocational education is thus virtually an obligatory part of the upbringing of the majority of young Germans. The remainder of the week during those years is spent as a trainee at a workplace under a qualified supervisor – a master craftsman (*Meister*) or someone with equivalent pedagogical qualifications

Table 2.3 *First degrees awarded by universities and higher education institutes in the United Kingdom and Germany, 1986–7, by main subject of study (thousands)*

	UK	West Germany(a)
Engineering and technology	16.4	26.4(b)
Science	27.1	12.9(c)
Medicine and health	7.5	12.2
Administrative, business and social studies(d)	29.8	45.7
Other professional and vocational studies(e)	6.0	9.2
Languages and arts	28.9	12.0
Education(f)	9.0	2.8
Total	124.7	121.2

Sources: *Education Statistics for the UK 1989*, p. 42; *Statistisches Jahrbuch 1989*, p. 356 (the German subject-classification has been rearranged to correspond with the British).
Notes:
(a) Degrees awarded by universities and *Fachhochschulen* (*Diplome* and corresponding qualifications, excluding teaching qualifications).
(b) Excluding architecture and town planning.
(c) Excluding geography.
(d) Includes economics, law, management, accountancy, psychology and geography.
(e) Architecture, town planning, agriculture, forestry, veterinary science.
(f) Excluding teaching qualifications (see p. 117, note 7).

– where a centrally approved rotation of tasks is followed as prescribed for that particular training occupation.

At their 'day release' vocational college, trainees study vocational subjects associated with their chosen career and, in addition, take further courses in general educational subjects (languages, mathematics, social studies); each of these broad groups of subjects – vocational and general – account for approximately half of the time spent in college. Intermediate and final examinations cover both specimen practical tasks (for example, a mechanic is required to make a metal item from an engineering drawing in a stated time; a commercial trainee is required to draw up a trial balance for a partnership's accounts) as well as written 'theoretical' work (to test understanding of the underlying general principles). The

Table 2.4 *Numbers passing vocational examinations at craft level in Britain, 1989, and Germany, 1988: mechanical, electrical and building trades*

Britain		Germany	
Occupation title (C&G ref no.)	No. passing	Occupation title (course ref no.)	No. passing
MECHANICAL			
Mechanical engineering (205)(a)(d)	2,400	Fitter (27)	35,200
Welding engineering (215)	100	Smith, solderer (24/25)	1,700
Sheet metal & thin plate (216)	400	Precision mechanic (2840)	2,000
Structural and thick plate (217)	200	General mechanic (2850)(b)	4,400
BTEC National Certificate(c)	5,600	Toolmaker (29)(d)	7,800
BTEC National Diploma(c)	2,400	Turner, etc. (22)	5,400
Total	*11,100*	*Total*	*56,500*
ELECTRICAL			
Electrical installation work (236)	5,300	Electrical installation (3110)	21,400
Electrical electronic craft studies (232)	1,300	Telecommunications (3120)	6,000
Electronics servicing (224)	1,300	Radio, TV, etc. (3151-9)	3,800
BTEC National Certificate(c)	6,000	Other electricians (in group 31)	9,500
BTEC National Diploma(e)	2,500		
Total	*16,400*	*Total*	*40,700*
BUILDING			
Brickwork and masonry (588)	6,000	Brickwork etc (44)(f)	8,100
Carpentry (585-7)	9,000	Carpentry (45, 50)	16,000
Plastering, tiling, heating installation (590-2, 595, 597)	900	Plastering, tiling, heating installation (48-9)	5,100
Painting and decorating (594)	2,300	Painting and related occupations (51)	11,200
Roadwork (614)	200	Roadwork (46)	1,900
Total	*18,400*	*Total*	*42,300*
Grand Total	***45,900***	***Grand Total***	***139,500***

Sources: *City and Guilds Examination Statistics 1988* (Part II or equivalent), *BTEC Awards 1988–89* (mimeo). *Bildung und Kultur 11.3, Berufliche Bildung 1989* (Statistisches Bundesamt).

Notes to table 2.4
(a) 1,996 on craft courses, 431 on maintenance courses (rounded down in table).
(b) Excluding *Handwerk* specialisations such as sewing-machine, office-machine and refrigeration mechanics; these totalled some 2,000.
(c) Estimate: BTEC statistical returns for this year show only a combined total for mechanical and electrical specialisations; on the basis of returns for 1985–6, when the numbers were separated, we have allocated half to each category.
(d) Toolmaking is not shown separately in this table for Britain, since it is a specialist course at Part III, taken after completing course no. 205 at Part II; the numbers are therefore already included in the latter total. Some 300 passed in Britain in 1988–9 in this specialisation.
(e) As for note (c) above, including those passing in courses specifically described as electrical and electronic.
(f) Excluding those shown in the published totals as passing the lower (or intermediate) level Phase 1 courses (to avoid double-counting with Phase 2).

examinations are externally set and externally marked, and passes in both written and practical tests are required for the award of the final qualification as a certified craftsman (*Fachmann*).

Two-year traineeships are available for a few occupations in Germany. In some occupations they form the first stage of the corresponding three-year course; but in others, including retailing and office work, the shorter courses are distinct and often taken by school-leavers with lower career ambitions – including those who have repeated a year at school and are thus subject to a shorter period of obligatory vocational schooling (the legal obligation is not for a fixed period, but ends at age eighteen).

Most of this will not be strange to anyone familiar with the traditional apprenticeship system in certain branches of British industry, such as engineering and building; what is remarkable in Germany – as in other parts of the Continent – is the way that approach has been developed to cover virtually the whole economy, and thus extends to the greater part of the workforce. This raises the issue of standards: has the very much greater proportion of youngsters attaining vocational qualifications led to a lowering of standards – in other words, has 'more meant worse'?

Comparisons of standards can be made only on the basis of what is required for particular occupations. Detailed comparisons by experts were therefore organised by the National Institute of examination papers and practical tasks set at the end of courses (and sometimes at the intermediate stage) for five important specimen occupational groups in Britain and Germany: mechanical craftsman, electrician, building craftsman, office worker and shop assistant. Specialist teachers and examiners at vocational colleges and at training boards in both countries cooperated in providing assessments of the standards and breadth of material covered. In choosing these five occupational groups we wished to cover, first, a fair spread of economic activity – not only manufacturing; second, not only occupations in which high technical skills are obviously required, but also some occupations in which the contribution of extended training may be less obvious; and third, some occupations in which male trainees are predominant and other occupations in which female trainees are predominant. Each of these occupational groups, as just listed, in reality consists of a number of related specialisations with substantial 'common core' elements. For example, related to the main qualification for mechanical craftsmen in Britain there are specialised qualifications in engineering maintenance, welding, sheet metal and thin plate, structural and thick plate; while in Germany the related qualifications cover fitters, smiths, solderers, precision mechanics, general mechanics, and so on. These specialisations cannot individually always be matched precisely between the two countries; but, taken as a group, they cover much the same broad occupational field of 'mechanical craftsmen', and there are sufficient common elements in the main specialisations to permit comparisons of scope and level of difficulty.

Comparisons for the 'male-dominated' occupations – mechanic, electrician, and building craftsman – are easier to summarise, and may be taken first. The standards expected in Germany in examinations at the end of their three-year vocational course (*Berufsabschlussprüfung*) were substantially similar to those expected in Britain at examinations such as Part II of City and Guilds. The latter were the relevant British examinations at the time the comparisons were made; since then the National Council for Vocational Qualifications has led to some modifications in the British qualifications, as will be discussed below. It remains important, nevertheless, that until very recently there was a clear similarity both in scope of material covered and in level of difficulty of vocational examinations at craft level in the two countries. That judgement was easier to make in the context of the availability – in addition to the main craft-level qualifications – of lower and higher recognised qualifications in both countries. Thus, in Britain there is a lower examination known as City and Guilds Part I, and a higher level for technicians (BTEC Higher); in Germany, the corresponding levels are provided by the intermediate vocational examinations (*Zwischenprüfung*) and the examinations for *Techniker* or *Meister*. These qualification ladders are more or less parallel in both countries, and made it easier to judge where equivalent levels lay.

Since the main craft qualification is awarded in both countries some three years after completing full-time compulsory schooling, say at ages eighteen to nineteen, it is perhaps not entirely surprising that broadly the same standard is aimed for in both countries (some differences will be noted shortly). Accepting that equivalence for the moment, the difference between the countries in these occupation groups can be judged from the numbers qualifying in 1988–9 detailed in table 2.4.

Overall, about three times as many attained craft qualifications in this fundamental group of occupations in Germany as in Britain. The gap was larger for qualified mechanics, where it reached a factor of five. That gap increased in the past decade, following persistent falls in Britain of those embarking on craft-engineering apprenticeships (a fall of over 50 per cent in that decade in numbers qualifying), combined with a rise in Germany of about a tenth.[9] The British decline in apprenticeships partly reflects the general decline in the output and employment of the engineering industry in Britain, which can be regarded as having now entered a vicious spiral – low skills leading to poor quality of products, lower export and home orders, lower employment, and low recruitment of trainees; but partly the decline in apprenticeships also reflects the opening of employment opportunities in certain categories of semi-skilled work which had previously been reserved for those who had served an apprenticeship. The latter reservation of work to those with full skill qualifications may have been justifiable in certain jobs in the past because of the technical complexity of the work; in others it had become no more than a restrictive practice. On the whole, however, there seems little doubt that the substantial decline in the numbers on mechanical apprenticeship courses from an initial low level must be regarded as an unhealthy lowering of the long-term technical capabilities of British industry.

In electrical occupations about two and a half times as many now qualify each year in Germany as in Britain. The decline in Britain in the numbers qualifying has been less severe than in mechanical occupations – a decline of only about a tenth in the past decade – while there has been a rise in Germany of about a fifth.[10] Amongst qualified construction workers, remarkably enough, there has been a substantial rise in Britain in the past decade – of about 60 per cent (from 11,000 a year to 18,000) while the German total has fallen by a quarter; as a result, the gap between the countries has narrowed, but remains substantial: twice as many now qualify each year in Germany as in Britain, compared with five times as many a decade ago.

Turning to the two 'female dominated' occupational groups, office work and retailing: a British reader might question at first whether extended programmes of training are necessary for very many engaged in such occupations. However, the persistent complaints received by British industry from customers at home and abroad relate not only to the technical quality of production, but also to organisational matters – keeping track of orders and stocks, late delivery, inadequate follow-through with information to customers: these complaints support a greater degree of training than at present given in Britain to those entering office occupations. The frequent complaints of lack of elementary professionalism amongst the generality of retailing staff similarly raise the question whether training in other countries is indeed more thorough than here.

It is precisely because the German approach – as of the other Continental systems that we shall survey – to educational preparation for these occupations differs so much from that now current in Britain, that it is worth describing in a little more detail. A fundamental difference is that trainees for such occupations in other countries are expected to progress during their training period not only in their vocational capabilities but also in their general education (as mentioned above, trainees elsewhere are usually required to pass final tests in their own language and in mathematics, for example, together with tests in the specific vocational subjects for their occupation). The development of a trainee's general education at those ages is regarded not only as an important aim in itself but also as helping to retain an 'open door' both to other occupations and to more advanced levels of qualification at which written communication and calculation become increasingly important. Indeed without the 'open door' to higher qualification levels, the attraction of a vocational course to a 16-year-old Continental youngster would be significantly reduced: it would be seen as an unpromising dead end rather than an alternative route to yet higher levels, including university-level qualifications.[11]

Training for office work in Germany follows, in broad structure, the same pattern as for the apprenticed trades familiar in Britain that were discussed above. The main route in Germany is via a three-year period of apprenticeship at work, with a nationally standardised rotation of tasks, combined with part-time (day-release) courses; there are also shorter full-time courses at commercial schools. A broad curriculum has been developed which aims for parity of esteem – at least in a formal sense – with qualifications in other occupations. In Britain courses in office work of a similar breadth are also available – such as the BTEC National Diploma in office studies – but most trainees in Britain for office work take narrower courses which specialise, for example, in correspondence or in book-keeping, but only rarely in both – as is the practice in Germany. The breadth of the approved German office-work courses may be illustrated by the following list of obligatory topics (specific examples in brackets are quoted from final examination papers): commercial practice (for example, dealing with bills of exchange); commercial correspondence (drafting and typing a letter to a supplier who has failed to deliver, reminding him of the purchaser's legal remedies); basic book-keeping; commercial arithmetic (dividing partnership profits in accordance with a partnership agreement).

Similar topics are touched on at English secondary schools at ages fourteen to sixteen by those pupils taking commercial subjects at GCSE; some of these courses are of a surprisingly high standard, where they are of a specialised nature. These courses are now broadening, partly under the influence of the National Curriculum. The aim of the German day-release courses at 16+ is, of course, distinctly higher than school-leaving standard. The German courses are intended to impart professional standards and professional mastery; it is the numbers attaining those levels that are our principal concern in our comparisons here.

A total of some 85,000 persons qualified in Germany in 1988 at the end of such three-year office-work courses; some three-quarters were female. This means that about one in five of all young women attained office-work qualifications at this level in Germany. The standards were judged comparable to those of BTEC qualifications at National Diploma level, with specialisation in office or secretarial skills; if we include National Certificates (which have a narrower curriculum than National Diplomas) as well as similar qualifications at these levels for 'private secretaries' awarded by the Royal Society of Arts, the London Chamber of Commerce and Industry, and Pitman's (their Secretarial Group Certificate), the total number qualifying at this level in Britain in 1989 totalled a mere 3,100 – that is, only about a thirtieth of the German total.[12]

We may attempt to swell the British total by including qualifications at the significantly less advanced level known as the BTEC First Diploma with specialisation in office studies; together with awards at equivalent levels from the other bodies mentioned, this would add a further 8,000.

Going further down that qualitative slope, we might also include 7,000 qualifying in Britain on narrower courses known as the BTEC First Certificate (usually only a one-year part-time course) and some 2,000 qualifying at comparable RSA levels. These additions bring the British total to 20,000. On the German side it would then be appropriate to include some 10,000 who qualified after two-year traineeships for clerical assistants (*Bürogehilfe*, as distinct from the *Bürokaufmann* qualification, which takes three years), bringing the German total to 95,000, which is still nearly five times the British total. In brief: we see that the great majority of those taking office-work qualifications in Germany do so on the basis of significantly broader and more advanced three-year courses of training; while in Britain the numbers qualifying are much lower, and their qualifications are based more often on shorter and narrower courses.[13]

Training for retailing in Germany, as for other occupations in the distribution sector, follows a very similar pattern to that just outlined for office work, that is, it is based mainly on two- or three-year traineeships with associated day-release courses. Two-year courses are taken more frequently in retailing than in other occupations, and account for nearly half the total number qualifying in that occupation; they lead to the basic level of qualified salesperson (*Verkäufer*). The longer three-year apprenticeship courses (*Kaufmann* – 'merchant', or shop manager) include a variety of specialised options intended, for example, for those wishing eventually to manage a shop on their own, to become a buyer in a larger store, or to work in foreign trade. A total of 110,000 obtained a qualification (after either two- or three-year courses of training) in this group of occupations in Germany in 1988; three-quarters were female, accounting for nearly one in four of all young women in the relevant age-group. Taking office work and retailing together, it is noteworthy that vocational qualifications in these two occupational fields are attained by nearly half of all young women in Germany.

In Britain the main nearest awards in distributive occupations, at a comparable level, are provided by BTEC through their National and First courses; related courses are provided by Pitman's (at their Level II) and by specialist retailing associations, such as drapers, hardware, furniture, fresh produce. The total number qualifying at these levels in Britain hardly reaches 2,000 a year – a mere 2 per cent of the German total. Other courses in these occupational groups have been developed more recently in Britain at a 'Foundation' or 'Pre-vocational' level by City and Guilds, the Royal Society of Arts and others; the stimulus for their development has often been the subsidy provided by the Youth Training Scheme for industrial trainees taking approved courses. Such lower-level courses may be welcomed as a foundation which may lead to training at higher levels; certificates are usually based on attendance at courses, rather than on any examination. The total number on such courses amounted to some 15,000 in 1990 – but even that is only a fraction of the numbers passing the much more substantial examined German courses in distribution.

Vocational training: some policy issues

This completes our outline of the main features in respect of which the German system of vocational training contrasts with that of Britain. We are now in a position to consider four detailed aspects relevant to current policy issues in Britain: the number of authorised training-occupations, mathematical standards in vocational courses, the testing of apprentices' vocational theory and practice, and the role of legal obligation to attend vocational courses.

First, the number of training occupations open to school-leavers in Germany, together with associated authorised curricula and qualifying examinations, is restricted to a total of about 380; the French, Dutch and Swiss have similar numbers. While this may seem more than ample, a considerably larger number has emerged from the plans of Britain's recently (1987) established National Council for Vocational Qualifications. For example, in mechanical engineering occupations alone, NCVQ planned to approve an immense number of combinations of specific 'Segments' – any six out of a menu of 250 – to qualify at craft level, compared with under fifty qualifications in this sector in Germany and France. This amplitude arises from a desire to make up a total 'qualification package' for each trainee close to the individual employer's specific requirements.[14] The grand total number of qualifications for all occupations was originally thought to be in the region of 1,000–2,000; but lower numbers (in the region of 700?) may emerge following debates and comparisons with the Continent.[15] The danger inherent in the British approach is that the qualifications thus become too specific and do not contribute sufficiently to the stock of transferable skills: it may suit the immediate interests of employers individually to have more specific skills, but it is not necessarily in the interests of employees, who ought to prepare for a possible change of jobs; nor would it promote the required increased flexibility of the economy.

The number of authorised training courses in Germany has been gradually reduced (from over 600 in the 1930s) to the present number in order to provide greater vocational breadth for the trainee; many courses (for example, in engineering) now share a common first year and sometimes also share much of the second year, with full specialisation taking place only in the final year. Some courses in the engineering group have been extended in the past decade to three and a half years to allow for greater breadth and specialised depth. Change of final specialisation by the trainee, and the acquisition of additional specialisations, have become easier on the basis of a broader initial training.

Second, the comparisons of standards in the two countries outlined above were based on the main 'craft-level' of qualification; we concluded that – at least as a first approximation – they could be regarded as much the same in the two countries. Looked at more closely, however, it has to be said that whenever mathematical skills were involved the standard expected in Britain was lower than in Germany. This was evident in both technical and commercial qualifications; for example, in electrical work – the interpretation of circuit drawings and the associated practical wiring of circuits

were at a significantly more complex level in Germany;[16] similarly, in retailing – long-standing complaints about arithmetical competence in Britain were reflected in remarkably elementary standards of questions in final test papers.[17] This raises broader issues as to whether standards of
mathematics in our secondary schools need to be revised; we return to this
issue in chapter 4 when we consider school-leaving standards in the two
countries.

Third, the German training system seems better in combining theory and
practice, that is, in linking instruction at college and training at work, and
in objectively testing attainments in both those aspects. A scheme of rotation for the main tasks at work is centrally approved in Germany for each
authorised field of training and, as mentioned, the trainee at work is under the supervision of a certified master-craftsman or equivalent. When it
comes to final examinations it needs to be emphasised that passes are required both in written tests and in practical tests, and both must be marked
by examiners who do not know the candidate. These are in addition to a
certificate of satisfactory performance during the candidate's traineeship
at the workplace.

In Britain externally marked written tests have long been familiar; but
externally marked practical tests have been rarer. An interesting exception
is provided by the building industry, which decided in the 1980s that independent practical tests had become essential; many trainees who had
received recognition as skilled workers were not performing well. Poor
workmanship included the following examples (listed at the time by the
Construction Industry Training Board):[18]

- difficulty in hanging a door within a reasonable tolerance (of the
  usually required 2mm gap);[19]

- failure to check whether their work was within stated tolerances;

- painting subject to runs, and poor masking;

- inability to interpret simple working drawings.

Following visits to Germany by a delegation from that Training Board,
practical tests were introduced in Britain (strictly, were 'reintroduced' – since
they had been used to some extent before 1970); but they were not made
obligatory (only about a third of those who passed written tests in construction trades took such practical tests in 1989).

It might have been hoped that the National Council for Vocational
Qualifications – as part of its new approach to these issues – would be in-
strumental in requiring rigorous independent testing of practical skills, combined with externally marked written tests; but that organisation set off

on a very different path. It requires practical competences to be demonstrated primarily – not to an independent examiner – but to the trainee's own normal workplace supervisor. Supervisors are sometimes subject to human failings; and for whatever reason (embarrassment, favouritism) may certify trainees as having satisfactorily carried out the requisite task when in reality that was not so. The consequent lack of reliability did not seem to weigh heavily with NCVQ; nor did the value of independent assessment as a means of promoting confidence in their qualifications and their marketability, and so promote the transferability of skills. In the same vein, the Council frowns on written tests, and on timed tests; these are regarded as irrelevant in relation to what a trainee will be expected to do during normal working life.

The view more often to be heard on the Continent, on the other hand, is that centrally set, externally marked written tests are an essential adjunct to practical tests and to certified workshop experience. Such written tests contribute to ensuring nationwide benchmarks for each occupation's standards (and thus contribute to transferability of skills and the marketability of qualifications); they enable a broader range of knowledge to be examined in the available time (and are thus more economical in costs of certification); they enable understanding of general principles to be tested (and so promote flexibility at work); and they recognise the need in an increasingly technologically complex economy for qualified personnel to have mastery of written communication. In addition, as previously mentioned, written tests help to keep the door open for an apprentice to aspire to higher levels of qualification. The 'new' British approach contains elements of a reversion to hoary time-serving traditions, when each master certified his own apprentice on the basis of his own judgement.

Fourth, we need to consider more closely the role of legal obligation in the vocational education of young persons. For many decades sporadic debates have taken place in Britain as to whether day-release to attend vocational schools should be made legally compulsory for school-leavers, more or less on the German pattern. The 1918 Education Act gave power to local education authorities to introduce local regulation to that effect; the best-known and longest surviving example was Rugby, where a Continuation School was established in 1920. Two years' part-time attendance was required after completing full-time schooling, and no local employer was permitted to employ a young person unless day-release was granted. The school was closed in 1969 following the raising of the general school-leaving age.[20]

The present legal position in Germany is more complex than it was until the mid-1970s. Until then all young persons not continuing in full-time education after the legal minimum of fifteen or sixteen (depending on the *Land*) were required to attend part-time vocational classes specific to their chosen apprenticeship or trainee-occupation at least until the age of eighteen, or older if their training continued to a later age; those who could not obtain a traineeship were required to attend part-time general vocational classes till eighteen. There were corresponding legal obligations on employers to provide day-release for all under-18s on their books. The present position, as it has evolved in most *Länder*, is that a single year of full-time vocational education can be substituted by under-18s in place of their longer obligation to attend part-time classes; after completing that full-time year they are permitted to be employed without restriction.[21] Only about a tenth of 16–17-year-olds attend such single-year full-time vocational courses, mostly because they were unsuccessful at the relevant time in finding an employer who was prepared to offer them training. Nearly half of that tenth take up a traineeship or apprenticeship in a later year, and then enrol on normal part-time specific vocational courses; thus, only one in about twenty of the age group fall outside the normal vocational training scheme.[22] In short, it seems that continuing economic and social pressures are such that those leaving full-time compulsory schooling in Germany at the minimum legal age continue to behave as if under virtual compulsion to seek an apprenticeship with accompanying attendance at a part-time vocational college till eighteen.

The implication perhaps is this: once training and vocational qualification are regarded as the part of the social norm, the prop of legal obligation can be taken away with negligible consequence – at least so far as has yet become evident. With the earlier maturation of teenagers, it is in any event difficult to enforce college attendance. Reliance needs therefore increasingly to be placed on adequate economic incentives, combined with effective pre-vocational education during the period of compulsory full-time schooling.

French full-time vocational colleges

Let us now outline – if only briefly, to keep within the limits of the present work – how four other advanced industrialised economies organise their vocational preparation. Three are European: France, the Netherlands and Switzerland; and one is a more recently industrialised non-European country, Japan. An adequate comparison with the United States is regrettably not possible, mainly because of that country's immense diversity and its lack of any nationwide system of intermediate qualifications.[23]

We begin with France. In contrast to the part-time vocational courses

of Germany, the French have come to rely increasingly on full-time vocational colleges. The option of qualifying via an apprenticeship, beginning
at the age of 15–16 and accompanied by part-time college attendance, was
followed by only a fifth of those qualifying at craft level in 1988. Occupations in which apprenticeship remains the predominant route to qualification in France are those where small firms predominate: they include food
preparation trades (bakers and butchers, with their well-known French
specialities – *pâtisserie* and *charcuterie*), hairdressing, and certain building occupations.[24] The final qualifying examinations are the same whether
the full-time college route or the apprenticeship route is followed.

The scope and level of difficulty of the French basic vocational qualifications are broadly similar to the qualifications for Germany just surveyed.
There are two varieties of French qualification, one with a greater practical content (the *Certificat d'aptitude professionnelle*, or CAP) taken by the
majority, and the other with a greater theoretical content (the *Brevêt
d'études professionnelles*, or BEP); these correspond broadly with craft and
technician ('Ordinary' level) qualifications in Britain.[25] Differences between
the two French varieties have narrowed over the years, and their amalga-
mation has frequently been discussed. Plans for the future are based on
increasing the theoretical and general elements in vocational courses combined with a much-heralded 'repackaging' of qualifications attained at 18+
under an increased variety of *Baccalauréats*. An increasing proportion of
students is expected to follow technician (BEP) courses, and craft (CAP)
courses are to be relegated to a minority who experience difficulty with
the technician level. There continues to be much debate and change in these
matters in France, with occasional suggestions that more youngsters would
do better on day-release apprenticeships as in Germany.[26]

At this point it is important to consider in what ways full-time and part-
time vocational instruction lead to differences in the mix of an apprentice's
actual competences. Though far from clear-cut, these matters are frequently
the subject of comment by those with extensive practical experience. It is
said that full-time vocational courses, even if accompanied by much practical work in college workshops, cannot provide the same thoroughness
of working experience as obtained by apprentices in their places of employment. Further, as far as general theoretical understanding is concerned,
it is valuable that part-time courses at college are interleaved with practical experience in the workplace under the supervision of a master-craftsman. That alternation helps the learning of general principles, and is especially important for those who have difficulties with a theoretically based
approach. In addition, apprentices have the advantage of seeing and participating in what needs to be done to ensure that customers' needs are

met fully, reliably and promptly; and they also experience the consequences of failing to meet customers' needs as well as a competitor does. Qualification on the basis of apprenticeship combined with a part-time college course thus has the advantage of bringing the trainee at an earlier age closer to the realities of the workplace and the constraints of the market.

Full-time courses, on the other hand, usually have a greater theoretical component in their studies, which may be to the long-term advantage of those aspiring to higher levels of responsibility and the planning of complex projects. Someone who has qualified after a full-time vocational course, may well require a further year or two of working experience before being considered fully fledged. Some youngsters are repelled by the very prospect of more full-time schooling; for them, an apprenticeship within the realities of a workplace environment may be better in fostering their practical competences and, as said, helps in developing associated theoretical understanding.

Because of the great variety of human abilities, and the variety of attainments and career ambitions of young persons, most countries find it advantageous to provide both part-time and full-time instructional routes to acquiring vocational qualifications; and both routes are to be found in most countries for most occupations. But countries differ characteristically in the preponderant use made of these alternative routes. The advantage of being able to produce *reliable* complex products, it is sometimes said in Germany, is connected with the stronger practical element in their predominant apprenticeship system; whereas French originality in design, it is said in France, is connected with the greater element of theoretical preparation provided by their full-time system of vocational instruction. There is probably more than an element of truth in both these generalisations; but reality is undoubtedly more complex, as we have to recognise in the light of Japanese experience to be surveyed below.

For our immediate purposes of understanding the French system of vocational preparation we have to note certain organisational features of their secondary schooling in relation to vocational courses available to school pupils from the age of fourteen. First, for many years France has provided a stratum of separate secondary vocational schools (*Lycées professionnels*); second, within many Comprehensive schools (*Collèges*) a vocational stream (*quatrième et troisième classes technologiques*) has been developed since the mid-1980s; third, there is a stratum of pre-apprenticeship classes attached to apprenticeship centres (*classes pré-professionnelles de niveau*, and *classes préparatoires à l'apprentissage*). These three vocational paths, taken together, were attended in 1991–2 by one in ten of all 14-year-olds, and one in six of all 15–16-year-olds.[27]

The curriculum for these vocational paths includes courses in both general and vocational subjects, and leads ultimately to examinations for the basic vocational qualifications mentioned above. Schooling in France is compulsory until sixteen, but most who have started on these vocational courses continue voluntarily for a further year or two to attempt the final qualifying vocational examinations. It perhaps again needs to be emphasised that even after the age of sixteen, in contrast to the approach in Britain, the French insist on examinations in general educational subjects to accompany all examinations in vocational subjects.

In contrast to the large Colleges of Further Education in Britain, usually catering for a very great range of occupations, French vocational schools tend to be specialised in particular occupational sectors and are relatively small (under 500 pupils on average).[28] Within each sector they provide courses which are broader in the early years, and lead in the final year to more specialised options and associated qualifying examinations (for example, within building schools there are courses leading to recognised craft qualifications in carpentry, painting and decorating, brickwork; and within commercial schools there are courses in insurance, book-keeping, retailing).

Dutch vocational secondary schools: early specialisation

The Dutch are similar to the French in a considerable reliance on full-time vocational secondary schools and colleges; in addition, and close to the German traditions, they legally require all 16- and 17-year-olds who have left full-time school to continue at part-time vocational colleges for one or two days a week. The details of Dutch part-time college attendance legalities vary according to training occupation and locality; the usual requirement is attendance at a vocational college for two days a week at age sixteen, and one day a week at seventeen.

About a third of all Dutch secondary pupils in 1988 attended a secondary school with a specialised vocational emphasis, the Junior Vocational Schools (*Lagerberoepsondenwijs*, or LBO for short). These schools are similar to *Lycées professionnels* in France in being specialised by broad occupational groups, for example, a single school, but differ in two respects. First, they provide four-year courses for a somewhat younger age group, namely 12–16-year-olds – rather than two- or three-year courses at 14–18 as in France; second, they do not lead to such a fine degree of occupational specialisation as in France, perhaps because courses finish at an earlier age (sixteen rather than eighteen). Vocational subjects enter the curriculum only in the final two years of Dutch secondary schooling, that is, from the age of fourteen; the initial two years are devoted entirely to general education, with syllabuses adapted to the ability of pupils at these schools and their likely future course of study. The difference between the Dutch and French curricula at comparable ages is thus less than may at first appear.

These Dutch vocational schools are thus similar, but on the whole more specialised than most English secondary technical (or 'central') schools as they developed until the 1960s, which pupils entered at age eleven or thirteen (depending on the local education authority) and received a combined general and vocational education.[29] Almost all such schools in Britain were submerged in the subsequent movement towards comprehensive schools catering for the whole ability range.

The decision to enter a Dutch vocational secondary school has to be made at a relatively early age, before twelve; if that school with its particular occupational specialisations proves unsuitable, it can be changed more easily in the first or second 'transitional' year of secondary schooling. There has for long been debate as to whether the Dutch differentiated secondary schooling system should be modified; and moves towards a multilateral form of secondary schooling have taken place since 1992. These involve delay in the choice of vocational specialisation till fourteen or fifteen, and easier transfer before that age between vocational and academic streams.

The standards reached at age sixteen on completing Dutch secondary vocational schools are remarkably high: in vocational subjects the standards correspond roughly to those reached at the end of the second year of a City and Guilds craft course, usually taken in England at about age eighteen.[30] Based on that foundation, most pupils then move on to specialised vocational courses at full-time two- to four-year intermediate technical colleges (MBO) or via an apprenticeship with continuing part-time attendance at college.

Switzerland

The vocational training systems of two other advanced, and highly interesting, economies – Switzerland and Japan – have been compared with Britain in a briefer way as part of the National Institute's research programme in this field; it is worth summarising here some of the more important similarities and differences that emerged. Switzerland's high real income derives not only from its well-known banking system, but also from the many branches of its manufacturing industry that are of extraordinarily high international repute – such as precision engineering, machine tools, pharmaceuticals. Switzerland's education and training systems are in many ways similar to Germany's: the proportion of its workforce attaining recognised vocational qualifications is probably even slightly higher than Germany's, and very distinctly ahead of Britain. University degrees in total are at much the same level as in Britain; but degrees in engineering and technology are as important in Switzerland as in Germany, and about 50 per cent ahead of Britain when related to size of workforce.

The Swiss system of vocational qualification is based on apprenticeship under a qualified *Meister* (someone who has passed his *Höhere Fachprüfung*), release from employment to attend college for 1–2 days a week, and final externally marked qualifying examinations. The Swiss do not impose any legal requirement on those who finish school at sixteen to continue at a vocational school on a part-time basis; nevertheless, some 78 per cent of 17-year-olds not in full-time education (54 per cent of the age-group) were engaged in apprenticeship schemes with part-time college attendance in 1990. Only 13 per cent at that age were outside any form of educational enrolment. There are undoubtedly strong socio-economic pressures in favour of vocational qualifications in Switzerland, with much unskilled work being left to immigrants admitted on short-term work permits. It is especially in occupations requiring only lower skill levels that the Swiss do not have as many employed with vocational qualifications as do the Germans: for example, in retailing 56 per cent in Switzerland have such qualifications, compared with 71 per cent in Germany (but a mere 22 per cent in the UK!).[31]

Japan

The increasingly advanced technology embodied in Japanese manufactured products, and their reliability, has raised that country in hardly more than a generation to a distinguished place amongst the world's industrial leaders. High educational standards have undoubtedly been fundamental in Japan's economic progress. Virtually everyone in Japan now attends some form of full-time schooling till the age of eighteen; what is important from the point of view of this chapter is that about a quarter of all 15–18-year-olds attend full-time vocational upper secondary schools.

Japanese vocational schools are similar to those described above for France and the Netherlands; that is, the schools are specialised in half a dozen broad occupational groups, and the curricula consist of both general and vocational subjects (including practical work, some of which may be in industry). The content and standards of the vocational courses are comparable to our BTEC National Diploma. Compared with Britain, about twice as many per head of the workforce in Japan complete vocational courses at age eighteen at that level in mechanical, electrical and electronic fields; in business studies the factor is nearly tenfold. The courses at vocational secondary schools may include highly specific trade tests administered by official certifying bodies (for example, gas welding technician, licensed book-keeper) – though more usually these specific tests are taken in industry.

Other pupils in the fifteen to eighteen age group continue with a general curriculum at senior high schools, which are stratified by ability on the basis of entrance examinations. After completing the latter schools about a third of the age group move on to universities, where over twice as many graduate in engineering per head of the workforce as in Britain – that is to say, closer to the German and Swiss proportions. A further tenth go on to various forms of senior technical colleges ('special training schools', *senshu gakko*) with standards close to our BTEC Higher Diplomas.

Different as the cultural background of Japan may be, and difficult as that makes it for Britain to draw any simple lessons from the experience of that country, it is remarkable that the proportions attaining vocational qualifications are now so close to those on the European Continent, and so very much ahead of Britain.[32]

Overview

We see that the countries surveyed above differ somewhat in the routes they provide for vocational preparation; but their common feature is that they provide substantive vocational preparation starting at earlier ages and for a greater proportion of the age group than in Britain. The vocational qualifications eventually attained by the active workforce are shown in a highly condensed form in table 2.5 for France, the Netherlands and Switzerland, in comparison with Britain and Germany (previously considered at the beginning of this chapter in table 2.1).[33] We see that some 7–11 per cent of the workforce in all five countries hold qualifications at university and higher vocational levels; at the technician level, the variation is from 7 to 19 per cent, with the Dutch more than compensating in their high proportion of technicians for a low proportion of graduates. It is again at the intermediate craft level of vocational qualification that Britain's 18 per cent appears deficient: the Netherlands has 38 per cent (but more at technician level, as just noted). France has made considerable progress at these intermediate levels in the last two decades and, with 33 per cent of the workforce so qualified, is now just over half-way between Britain and the Netherlands.

Table 2.5 *Vocational qualifications of the workforce in Britain, France, Germany, the Netherlands and Switzerland, selected years 1988–91 (percentage of all economically active persons)*

	Britain 1989	France 1988	Germany 1988	Nether-lands 1989	Switzer-land 1991
University degrees(a)	11	7	11	8	11
Intermediate vocational qualifications	25	40	63	57	66
Of which:					
Technician(b)	7	7	7	19	9
Craft(c)	18(d)	33	56	38	57
No vocational qualifications(e)	64	53	26	35	23
Total	100	100	100	100	100

Sources: Estimates based on national Labour Force Surveys, including special tabulations prepared for NIESR; national qualifications reclassified to common basis as far as possible. For details on France, see the article by Steedman in *National Institute Economic Review,* August 1990; Netherlands, Mason *et al., ibid.,* May 1992; Switzerland, H. Hollenstein, National Institute Discussion Paper no. 54, September 1982, and work in progress by Bierhoff *et al.* at the Institute.
Notes:
(a) For Britain, includes professional qualifications of degree standard. For Netherlands, includes HTS diplomas and university education of three years or more.
(b) For Britain, includes basic qualifications excluded in other countries (see text), that is, City and Guilds Part I and above; BTEC National and equivalent; apprenticeships (NVQ level 2 and above; see (d)). For France, CAP and BEP. For the Netherlands MBO diplomas (apart from HTS) and half of all LBO diplomas (corresponding to those at levels C and D, and half of those at level B; see text). For Germany, *Berufsabschluss.* For Switzerland, includes also half of those completing lower-level qualifications based on 1–2 year traineeship course (*Anlehre*).
(d) Of which approximately 9% at City and Guilds Part 2 and equivalent (NVQ level 3), and 8% at City and Guilds Part 1 and equivalent (NVQ level 2).
(e) Only general education (below university level). For Britain, includes those with GCSE or A–levels, but without vocational or university qualifications. For the Netherlands includes half of LBO diplomas (half of those at level B and all at level A), and those without LBO diplomas; for Switzerland, includes half of *Anlehre* qualifications.

The proportion without vocational qualifications, conversely, is highest in Britain at 63 per cent: Switzerland, Germany and the Netherlands provide, broadly speaking, almost the same contrast with Britain in this respect, with only 26 and 38 per cent vocationally unqualified. As between the Netherlands and Germany, these figures indicate a somewhat greater problem of under-qualification in the Netherlands; this is reflected in a greater current concern with reforms of education and training in relation to low attainers in that country than in Germany. Despite recent progress, the problem of the under-qualified in France is greater still, and closer to that of Britain; ambitious targets have been announced there based on retaining four-fifths of all young persons in full-time schooling till the age of eighteen to attain various types of *Baccalauréat*.

By the standards of these industrialised countries, Britain thus seems clearly anomalous in the low proportion of its workforce that has received systematically organised vocational preparation and attained formally examined vocational qualifications. Our task in the next chapter is to examine the consequences for the organisation and efficiency of production.

3 Productivity and its determinants: case studies

Comparisons of matched samples of plants

An economy with a better-educated and better-trained workforce may be
expected to produce more efficiently: that proposition hardly needs elaboration at a general level. But there remains an important need to understand the detailed practical links between training and productivity – not
least in relation to advanced industrialised economies amongst which the
extent of training differs as greatly as described in the previous chapter.
Policies to improve training depend on a better understanding of those
links: we need to be clear on whether productivity advantages manifest
themselves significantly through, for example, more rapid working by
better-trained personnel, or perhaps through lower reject ratios; we need
to know which levels of productive personnel (operatives, foremen, supervisors, etc.) are particularly deficient in training, and the extent of those
deficiencies; and we need to consider whether productivity advantages
might simply be the result of choosing better machinery.

To cast light on these matters, a series of matched samples of manufacturing plants in Britain and the Continent were systematically visited in
the past decade by the National Institute. A fair spread of industries was
covered: metalworking, woodworking, clothing manufacture, food manufacture; a service sector – hotels – was examined in the same way. Most
of the comparisons were between Britain and Germany; others included
the Netherlands and France. The object of this chapter is to survey this
series of comparisons *taken as a whole*, and of the conclusions to which
they point (previously only the findings for the comparisons of individual
industries have been published, as each set was completed). We begin by
outlining how those industries and the firms within them were selected;

but a preliminary word is necessary on the nature of present-day international competition in manufactured products and the role of product quality.

Quantity and quality of output

International competition in manufactures today very often consists of competition in the reliability of products and their longevity, together with whatever contributes to a product's 'fitness for purpose', rather than simply competition in the delivered price of identical varieties. In measuring aggregate changes in productivity over time for a single country, official statisticians – with limited resources available for statistical development work – have in practice not been able to do very much to allow for quality changes. It has now, however, become familiar, as a result of careful US investigations, that statistical estimates of the growth of national real output are probably on balance slightly underestimated (perhaps by 1–2 per cent a year cumulatively), since gradual changes in quality that take place over time have not been brought into account; for the same reason, estimates of inflation must be expected to be slightly too high.[1]

If such worries arise within a single country, the quality differences associated with productivity comparisons between more and less advanced countries deserve even greater attention. While no doubt there are exceptions, on the whole it seems likely that higher-quality products tend to be produced in wealthier countries, as a result of higher local demand by those who can afford expensive varieties and the development of specialised local skills to meet those demands. Differences in average levels of quality between one country and another are therefore likely to be of a greater order of magnitude than those that national-income statisticians – estimating changes in one country's output between this year and last year – feel justified in overlooking. We shall need to refer to issues connected with quality at several points in describing the National Institute's empirical comparisons of productivity based on visits to matched plants; the issue needs mentioning at the outset to explain why a fair degree of empirical detail forms an essential part of what follows.

Industries selected for comparison

A total of over 160 establishments were visited in the course of the Institute's researches in the period 1983–91. Over seventy were in Britain, sixty in Germany and thirty in other countries; their industrial distribution is set out in table 3.1. The choice of the four particular manufacturing industries may seem not unjustified on the simple ground that it is valuable

Table 3.1 *Matched samples of plants in Britain and other countries taking part in the NI international comparisons, 1983–91, by industry and year of visit, typical products, size of plant, and number of plants in each comparison*

Industrial group (and year of study)	Typical products	Size-range of plants (employees)(a)	Number of plants studied in				
			Britain	Germany	Nether-lands	Other countries	Total
Engineering (1983-4)	Springs, drills, vehicle components	50-500	16	16	0	3(b)	35
Engineering (1990-1)	do.	100-200	12	0	9	0	21
Wood furniture (1986-7)	Fitted kitchens	150-350	9	8	0	0	17
Clothing (1987-8)	Women's skirts, jackets, suits	30-250	12(c)	10	0	0	22
Food manu-facturing (1989-90)	Biscuits	50-400	10	6	5	6(d)	27
Hotels (1988-9)	Accommo-dation in middle-range large-city hotels	20-100(e)	14	24	5(f)	0	43
Totals			73(c)	64	19	9	165

Notes:
(a) Approximate size range of plants covering half or more of total employment in all countries (except for hotels, see footnote (e)).
(b) USA.
(c) Plus eight small sub-contract clothing firms in Britain.
(d) France.
(e) Number of hotel bedrooms.
(f) Associated comparisons by Sandra Lunt (student at Polytechnic of North London).

to investigate a range of basic materials which today are subject to factory transformation – metals, wood, cloth, foodstuffs. Comparisons of a service activity, the provision of hotel facilities, are also of obvious interest to supplement comparisons of manufacturing; with less scope for mechanisation, it may be expected that international differences in productivity in services are smaller: we wished to check whether this is really so.

But perhaps the more important underlying reason why such a range of industries is of interest is that *different average skill levels* are typically required by each of them. The industries may be ranked, in a rough common-sense way, by skill level in the order given: metalworking usually requires greater precision and more training than woodworking, which in turn requires greater precision than the manufacture of clothing or foodstuffs; and most hotel services might seem to require even less in the way of training. Such a ranking by skill levels – rough as it undoubtedly is – reflects our central concern with tracing the relative productivity consequences of various levels of training, particularly of intermediate grades of personnel. The varying mix of skill levels raises questions as to whether the higher skill endowments characteristic of some countries are reflected equally in all the industries of those countries, or whether international productivity differences differ among these industries.

To cast light on international differences in the *selection* of modern machinery, on differences in the *adaptation* of machinery to the specific product and process requirements of each firm, and on differences arising in *maintenance* and running-in of new machinery, discussions were also held with specialist machinery suppliers for each industry. Machinery suppliers often sold to customers in several countries, and were able to add their own experience on how skill differences among customers in different countries affected installation and maintenance problems. Similarly, to help in comparing the initial attainments of trainees and the standards of their final qualifications, visits to colleges for the training of craftsmen and technicians for each industry were undertaken. The total number of these discussions with machinery suppliers and colleges usually exceeded the number of plants visited in each industry.

Sizes of plants selected for comparison

To ensure that the comparisons yielded results that could be treated as relevant to the greater part of the workforce, the most difficult and important decision was the selection of the sizes of the sample plants to be visited: they needed to be broadly representative of each industry and at the same time serve to highlight differences between the countries. Limitations on research resources inevitably required that the number of plants in the samples be kept small. Plants vary considerably in size, and thus in the associated number of managerial tiers as well as in their employment of technical specialists. A fully representative size-range of plants, even within a narrowly defined industry, would lead to undue variation and to problems of comparability between countries. It is undoubtedly more convenient for researchers to deal only with the largest firms, especially those having international connections, since such firms have sufficient inter-mediate tiers of management to deal with 'public relations' and research enquiries of this sort; but the skill needs of the very largest firms and their problems do not necessarily mirror those of average sized firms. Large firms are also more often engaged in mass production or large-batch production, in which much repetitive (short-cycle) work is carried out by personnel experienced in only a limited number of operations, and who see less need for broader vocational qualifications. Smaller firms, on the other hand, tend to have a greater need for broadly skilled persons who can competently lend a hand to a wide variety of production and maintenance tasks; for that reason smaller firms, cooperating with local technical colleges, provide a good training ground for apprentices, especially those hoping subsequently to set up in business on their own.

In the light of these considerations, the sample was chosen in the first place from the central half of the size distribution of total employment for each industry, as recorded in the Censuses of Production or allied statistics; that is to say, we generally excluded the smallest and largest plants – those that were below the size accounting for the bottom quarter of employment in each industry, and those above the size accounting for the top quarter. To ensure that plants of comparable size in each country were included, the range was then sometimes stretched – usually only a little – to provide sufficient overlap between countries; the final range of sizes thus usually covered somewhat more than the central half of employment in each industry. A very much larger research programme would be needed to include a full range of plant sizes; that may be justified in the years to come but, at this stage, it would have introduced into the comparisons too many complexities associated with the operation of the very largest and very smallest firms.

The consequence was that most plants in these comparisons were in the range of 50–300 employees, as shown in table 3.1.[2] The sample of hotels was chosen on the basis of number of hotel rooms (since that is how the available national statistics were compiled) and were similarly chosen from the middle of the size range.

The selection of individual plants was based on trade directories, followed by initial phone calls to elucidate employment size and the precise range of products manufactured. Some limitation in the choice of plants to those producing similar and characteristic products in each country was necessary to facilitate cross-country comparability; relatively simple products were chosen (such as: small coil springs in engineering, women's skirts in clothing manufacture) so that processes, skills and throughput rates could more readily be compared. Typical products chosen for each industry are shown in the second column of table 3.1. Of plants invited to participate, over half agreed to do so. Those agreeing may have been among the more successful; but any ensuing biases may be expected to be similar in each country, and thus not affect too much the observed differences between countries in productivity and related matters that are our concern here.

Having described the basis on which the Institute's matched samples of plants were chosen, we are ready to present our findings; this will be done in the following order. Average productivity differences between countries in the chosen samples of plants is described industry by industry in the following section. That section begins with productivity and quality differences in engineering, which are described in some detail; furniture and clothing are then considered in a more summary way. In food manufacturing, quality differences were put under closer scrutiny and an attempt made to evaluate such differences in money terms. We then turn to productivity differences in the service sector examined, namely, hotels. Following this the next section summarises our observed international differences in machinery and its state of maintenance, and we then describe the more noticeable ways in which skill levels affected relative productivity in the industries examined. Finally, we reflect on changing priorities in promoting higher productivity.

Productivity differences

Engineering

Six fairly comparable products were matched in the British and German engineering plants that were sampled: screws, springs, two varieties of hydraulic valves and two varieties of drill bits [8]. Productivity calculations were based on actual (not merely theoretical or 'standard') outputs per unit of time, that is, including downtime for tool-setting and tool-changing, and for material loading, and so on. Depending on how the production process was laid out and how records were kept, sometimes output rates for a single important operation in the production sequence were compared; in others, output rates for a combined series of operations were compared; in yet others, the total numbers of completed products were compared. Outputs were then related to the number of worker-hours directly employed in the sequence of operations covered.

Average productivity for these six engineering products was 63 per cent higher in the German than in the British plants (with a sampling error of ±9 per cent). This gap is somewhat greater than, but statistically consistent with, an estimate of about 50 per cent derivable from Censuses of Production for metalworking trades.[3] The productivity differentials for the various products lay in the range of 10–130 per cent advantage for Germany; variations in measured differentials were probably due partly to the undue simplicity or imperfections of our measurements and partly to genuine variability of efficiencies among plants within each country. No relation was observed with any obvious characteristics of the products, such as their complexity.

Several aspects of our findings deserve comment. First, in such simple products it might have been expected that only narrow productivity differentials between the two countries would be evident at the shop-floor level; much of the aggregate difference between the countries, it might be thought, would be evident only in complex and sophisticated products where, for example, better manufacturing design would lead to several operations being carried out simultaneously, or better marketing would lead to longer runs of standardised varieties. Such factors undoubtedly play an important part in the total productivity difference between the countries as a whole; it is therefore the more remarkable that differences in productivity of such a magnitude should emerge at the level of shop-floor productivity in these relatively simple products.

One must not, however, forget the role of international competitive pressures. If producers of such simple products are to survive in advanced countries at the higher wage levels that have evolved there, they can do so only if their productivity in those products is correspondingly high. At the time these comparisons were made, pressures were evident in Britain and Germany from developing countries which were successfully producing standard varieties, and were able to supply them in bulk quantities at low prices; surviving producers in advanced countries were obliged to raise their productivity, or shift their product range towards specialised varieties requiring greater skills. At the time of our visits some of the sampled firms in both countries were well advanced in modifying their product range, while others were struggling; but an air of despondency was encountered more often in the British than in the Continental firms we visited. An extreme view, not untypical of the wider problems of machinery maintenance in Britain (discussed further below), was expressed by one director: with faster and more modern machines, 'there is usually more to go wrong . . . the faster the machines work, the sooner the job is completed and the more setting will be required', leading to difficulties in maintaining smooth and efficient production. Similar views were not encountered in Germany.

Second, when examining the actual products made by sampled firms in the two countries, it soon became evident that the German firms tended to make products that were technically somewhat more advanced and of higher quality. To give some examples: in trying to match specific types of screw, it was found that the basic standard types made in Britain – and which had initially been thought suitable for international comparison – were no longer produced in Germany because of competition from the Far East; it was thus necessary to base comparisons on special – more expensive – types produced in both countries. Similarly, in matching the hydraulic valve taken from the main part of the British range, it was apparent that the matched German plant produced a broader and more specialist range of products – that is, on the whole, a more expensive range.[4] Conversely, a metal pressing received from one of the German sample plants could not readily be matched in Britain because of its complexity (a British plant in the matched sample that was approached hoped – but could do no more than hope – to be able to produce this type in the future). Our comparisons therefore must be suspected of not reflecting the full extent of the German productivity advantage.

Third, much was said to the investigators of greater standardisation and longer runs in Germany; for example, it was said that 'a German carmaker would design one spring for which its British competitors would need four kinds'. Nevertheless, for the particular engineering products compared here, sizes of batches were similar in the two countries. This is not to say that standardisation is unimportant: on the contrary, the themes of the Warner report (1977) on the need for more standardisation in British engineering were frequently heard in the course of these interviews – the need to eliminate 'dual working' to metric and imperial standards; the need for more careful initial design to incorporate readily available standard components, rather than purpose-made, components; and the benefits that would in due course ensue from larger orders for standard components.[5] However, the Institute's comparisons indicated that, even when batches of comparable size were made in the two countries, there was still a fundamental difference in productivity.

Finally, an apparent reservation that attaches to our measures of productivity is that they were based on direct labour only, and ignored indirect labour. This is unlikely to be a serious reservation, however, since earlier studies have suggested that indirect labour has been lower in other countries than in Britain.[6]

A subsequent sample of engineering plants in Britain was compared by the National Institute with matched Continental plants in 1991, this time in the Netherlands. In the seven years since the previous comparisons with Germany, British engineering had suffered a serious drop in total employment (of the order of 30 per cent); surviving firms in Britain had improved their productivity, and the productivity gap with the Continent had narrowed. Nevertheless, average productivity in the matched Dutch sample was still some 36 per cent higher than in the British sample.[7] In respect of the ability to produce specialised higher-quality products, the contrast between Britain and the Continent was still significant, if not quite as great as previously.

Wood furniture

The production of fitted kitchen cabinets – an important branch of the wood furniture industry – was compared in Britain and Germany by the National Institute in 1986–7 [9]. German manufacturers in this industry had established a postwar reputation for high-quality products, having started from an early recognition of a technical development, namely, that the future raw material of the furniture industry would no longer be natural wood, but chipboard with laminated plastic surfaces. This was a cheaper and much more uniform material – without natural variations requiring individual attention – and was much more suited to large-scale factory-production techniques. By the beginning of the 1980s an important divergence had developed between the two countries' producers in marketing aims and manufacturing processes: British producers aimed predominantly for the DIY flat-pack middle to lower market, based on large-batch production, while German producers specialised in high-quality completely-assembled rigid cabinets made to customers' individual orders.

The individuality of products demanded by customers of the furniture industry might be expected to limit the scope for productivity improvements arising from the application of modern manufacturing techniques. Nevertheless, statistics from the Censuses of Production for 1993 indicated that Germany had achieved a productivity advantage relative to Britain in the furniture industry at least as high as in manufacturing as a whole (over 60 per cent higher in Germany than British furniture production, compared with 50 per cent in manufacturing as a whole).

In trying to understand – with the help of visits to sample firms – the sources of Germany's higher productivity in the furniture industry, a central production process was chosen for closer examination, namely the main operations involved in making the basic panels for the carcase of a kitchen cabinet. This involved, first, cutting down a large panel of pre-surfaced chipboard to rough size; second, a cut to precise size; third, applying a decorative and protective strip to the raw edges of the panel; fourth, drilling holes to receive shelf supports and screws.

Average output *per machine line* was found to be only 6 per cent higher per hour in Germany; the important difference was in manning levels which, for similar machine lines, were just over twice as high in Britain as in Germany. Consequently, output *per employee* on these four processes taken together was about 2.3 times higher in Germany than in Britain. This was despite the fact that German firms produced a more varied and higher-quality product. It would be wrong to jump to the conclusion that a productivity gap at this high level characterised *all* processes in the German furniture industry; rather, processes of this kind can be mechanised and put under the control of skilled personnel, and such processes contribute disproportionately to the higher productivity of the industry taken as a whole.

Clothing

The clothing industries of both Britain and Germany have faced severe competition in the past generation from low-wage developing countries; under these pressures, differences developed between the clothing industries of both these countries which, as we shall see, are structurally similar to those just described for the furniture industry.

Matched samples of plants producing women's outerwear were visited in the two countries by the National Institute in 1987–8 [10]. At that time both countries' clothing industries were much the same size in terms of total employment (some 220,000 employed in each country, of whom 80 per cent were female); and employment in both countries had contracted to a similar extent in the preceding decade, by about a third. The major contrast immediately observed on visits to British and German clothing plants related to quality of products. The survival of German clothing manufacture was based, not on a wider application of mass-production principles to standard varieties, but rather on producing small batches of high-quality goods in great variety; British firms, on the other hand, depended to a great extent on manufacturing long runs of standard items.

Both countries have an immense range of clothing producers, each firm having its individual strengths and specialisations; but the contrast just mentioned – even if subject to detailed qualification – is central to any present-day overall comparisons between these countries' industries. The typical length of production run in women's outerwear in Germany was 150–300 garments; in Britain the length of run was more variable, but in the majority of plants visited was about a hundredfold greater – in the region of 15,000 garments. In Germany such long runs were virtually unheard of. As the study progressed, the original British sample of eight plants was extended to include four plants making medium and higher-quality garments to match the quality of product seen in Germany; these additional plants manufactured in batches of some 300 garments, much as in Germany. However, such plants were not typical of British production.

At the risk of simplification, three differences may be mentioned to illustrate the higher quality and styling that typified German clothing production. First, the German product (dresses, jackets, suits) consists of more separate pieces, and has more darts and tucks, to form a 'structured' and 'tailored' garment with more shape; second, it is more often made of checked or patterned material, requiring greater skill in cutting and joining to ensure that the pattern aligns; third, it includes more decorative stitching and other cutting details (for example, pockets diagonally set in) to provide styling interest and variation. The British garment, on the other hand, is more often made of fewer constituent pieces, it is made of plain materials, and has less decorative stitching. Only some dozen companies in the whole of Britain (so the Institute's observers were told by trade experts) had sufficient skilled employees to undertake work comparable in quality of workmanship to that taken for granted in the German clothing industry.

The number of garments produced per employee in the plants visited in the two countries varied, not surprisingly, according to type and quality of garment – from an average of just under one garment a day per employee for top-quality suits, to fourteen a day for blouses produced in very long runs. Taking averages of all the plants visited, without regard to quality and type of product, only a small difference was apparent: British plants produced just under five garments a day per employee while German plants produced just over five. The remarkable point however is that the higher German work content could be incorporated in the same number of garments as produced by the British plants, and that it could be done while working with much shorter production runs.

The German plants employed slightly fewer machinists per garment and, in addition, the ratio of other direct and indirect workers to machinists was lower: for every one machinist there was an average of half an additional direct or indirect worker in Germany, whereas in Britain there was an average of one additional worker for every machinist (direct workers other than machinists are, for example, cutters, pressers, fusers, finishers; indirect workers are those employed in administration, supervision, examining).

Though the plants compared were all producing women's outerwear, the considerable variety of garment types inevitably clouds the precision of any assessment of relative productivity. To obtain a better indication, plants accounting for half the original samples in each country were selected as producing garments of more closely comparable type and quality. In these plants it was found that Germany produced roughly twice as many garments per employee-hour as Britain. The plants omitted in this comparison were all producing women's outerwear, but of a less comparable sort: the omitted British plants mainly produced highly standardised products in very long runs, while the omitted German plants tended to produce 'model' garments in very short runs, the most successful of which were often subsequently produced on a larger scale by sub-contractors abroad.

Food manufacturing

The transfer of food preparation from home to factory – modern as that process may sound – has in reality been a long and gradual process, in which the traditional miller and village baker were among the early starters. The pace of transfer has accelerated in recent decades with improvements in food-preservation techniques and – more important than often realised – with the extension of branding and advertising by food manufacturers. The international comparisons of matched food-manufacturing plants carried out by the National Institute were deliberately based on a very simple product – biscuits – in the hope that productivity could be measured subject to fewer reservations, and in the hope that factors contributing to productivity differences could more easily be identified. Simple as that product might seem when compared to alternative manufactured foods, it was still found that quality mix differed substantially between countries, and inter-country differences in average quality needed to be brought into account explicitly.

The biscuit industry is now highly automated: production starts with automatic dough-mixing machinery and biscuit-forming machinery, followed by conveyor lines which take the product through long tunnel ovens, followed by automatic high-speed wrapping machinery. It is thus akin to modern continuous process industries which require not so much craft-skilled personnel as in the industries surveyed above, but personnel with technician-type skills able to monitor the satisfactory working of machinery, and able to make adjustments to allow for the considerable and inevitable variation in raw materials (for example, moisture content of flour) and in processing conditions (ambient temperatures). Unskilled personnel have a role mainly at the final packing stage.

Plants in four countries – France, Germany, the Netherlands and Britain – were visited in 1989–92 by National Institute researchers.[8] With few exceptions, each sample plant produced a variety of products in a variety of wrappings: the variative was, for example, from the plainest types (Morning Coffee, Marie) made with cheap fats and wrapped in a single plastic film, to multi-layer biscuits made of butter dough, cream-filled or chocolate-coated, double-wrapped in plastic film (to improve preservation) and then packed in printed cartons (cartons reduce risk of breakage, and can provide better printed sales appeal).

If labour productivity is measured simply in terms of tonnage produced per employee-hour – that is, ignoring quality differences – the Dutch sample of plants produced 15 per cent more than the British sample, the French sample about the same as the British, and the German sample – surprising as it might seem – produced 20 per cent less than the British sample.

A rough allocation of each country's production to three quality grades – basic, medium, elaborate – is set out in table 3.2. This was derived from the estimated proportions of each quality grade produced at the plants visited, but based – as was convenient in interviewing – on each country's concepts of quality grades. It is clear that Britain produced a greater proportion of what it considered were basic grades, Germany a greater proportion of elaborate grades, while the Netherlands and France lay between these extremes. As far as could be judged by a panel of tasters at the Institute, basic grades were in reality very similar in the four countries, but products classified to medium and elaborate grades covered a broader range of qualities. Different boundary lines had been drawn by producers in each country when they described their better-class products; for example, products usually classed in Germany as 'medium' grade were closer to those classed as 'elaborate' grade in Britain. This was reflected in the relative prices compiled for each country's product grade by the Institute's researchers, based on products observed in the plants visited; they are also shown in table 3.2 in the form of price ratios with the basic grade set as 100 for each country.

Price variations between quality grades are clearly enormous, varying by a factor of four in Britain, France and the Netherlands, and by six in Germany: the issue of quality differences is thus far from a matter of minor importance. An index of the average quality produced in each country can be calculated by weighting these price ratios by the proportions of the different quality grades produced in each country. This led to the estimates shown in the penultimate row of the table: the average biscuit produced in the Netherlands has a 15 per cent higher quality content per unit of weight than the average British biscuit, the French average is 30 per cent higher than the British, while the average biscuit produced in Germany is a very much more elaborate confection – selling at 2–3 times the retail price of the average biscuit produced in Britain.

Such large differences in the quality content of products clearly need to

Table 3.2 *Distribution of quality grades of biscuits and their relative prices in Britain (GB), Germany (D), France (F) and the Netherlands (NL), 1991*

Grade	Examples	Output share(a)				Price ratios(b)			
		GB	D	F	NL	GB	D	F	NL
Basic	Morning coffee; Marie (simple packaging)	40	15	20	35	100	100	100	100
Medium	Sandwich cream (medium quality); chocolate-coated on one side	55	55	70	50	200	430	220	210
Elaborate	Marzipan filling; nutty doughs; fully chocolate-coated (elaborate packaging, usually carton)	5	30	10	15	360	630	420	350
Average quality based on retail prices(c)						100	260	130	115
Average quality based on ex-factory prices(d)						100	180	120	110

Notes:
(a) Based on rough allocation of output of plants visited in the National Institute's comparisons.
(b) Based on retail prices of packets mainly of 250g (occasionally 125–450g, with proportionate adjustments); price of basic grade set at 100 for each country.
(c) Average of the three price-ratios for each country, weighted by output-proportions shown on left-hand side of table, expressed as index with GB = 100.
(d) Based on average value of sales per ton less cost of raw materials (derived from Censuses of Production), converted at a 'PPP exchange rate' for biscuits derived from the Institute's compilation of prices for this enquiry.

be brought into account in any comparisons of productivity. To do so simply on the basis of retail prices would, however, probably go too far, since products of a higher quality usually incorporate both higher retail margins (because of lower rates of stock turnover, greater element of retail service), and more expensive ingredients. A more complex calculation of average value-added in the factory was therefore carried out based on ex-factory sales prices, after deducting costs of raw materials (this information was derived from each country's Census of Production or related enquiries). Rather than rely on currency exchange rates to convert value-added in each country's monetary unit to a common denominator, an 'own

Table 3.3 *Quality-adjusted measures of productivity in biscuit production in Britain, Germany, France and the Netherlands, 1991*

	Physical output per employee-hour	Quality index per unit of output	Quality-adjusted productivity
Britain	100	100	100
Germany	80	180	145
France	105	120	125
Netherlands	120	110	135

commodity' exchange rate was calculated based on retail prices of closely matched grades of basic and medium grades of biscuits (the top 'elaborate' grades varied too much to form a reliable component of such a calculation). The results of this calculation, shown in the final row of the table, slightly moderate the previous quality ratios. They now suggest that the real value of the *average* biscuit produced in the Netherlands was some 10 per cent higher than in Britain, France was 20 per cent ahead; German quality – remarkably enough –– was still as much as 80 per cent ahead of Britain.

Combining differences in tonnage produced per employee in each country with differences in average quality, as derived in the preceding paragraph, leads to the quality-adjusted measures of productivity shown in table 3.3. The three Continental countries are now seen as all producing roughly a third more per employee-hour than the British producers, with Germany slightly ahead of the other two Continental producers. It is also worth noticing that more of the international differences seem attributable to higher-*quality* products than to producing just a greater *quantity* of basic products more efficiently.

Hotels

It might well be thought that international differences in productivity are likely to arise less in service sectors than in manufacturing, since manufacturing provides greater scope for advanced technology, for production on a large scale, and hence for the exercise of specialised skills. Economic commentators on productivity in services often also cite, and not entirely by way of anecdote, their experience of men's haircuts – which seem to take twenty minutes irrespective of country, and irrespective of whether the barber uses scissors or electric clippers. In advanced industrial countries the total number of persons employed in services now increasingly tends to exceed the numbers employed in manufacturing; it is thus clearly important to investigate whether international productivity differences of the magnitude observed in manufacturing industries, such as those surveyed in the preceding pages, are evident also in services.

Measuring real output in services, so as to yield figures that are internationally comparable, is more difficult than in manufacturing: it is less easy to identify and define standard grades of particular services, and it is difficult to measure the total number of equivalent standard-grade units produced (one need only think of the variety of ladies' hairstyles, of restaurant meals, or of hotel grades). Approximations made by National Accounts statisticians in individual countries in deriving measures of real output in services may be adequate for their purposes of providing an overall assessment of year-to-year movements for their economy; for example, changes from year to year in the real output of the hotel sector may be satisfactorily based on changes in the total number of guest nights spent in a country's hotels. But for international comparisons of productivity something more precise is required which, to follow this example, takes account of international differences in the average quality of hotel services.

The hotel sector was chosen by the National Institute for such a closer comparison based on matched samples in Britain and Germany [1]. It is a large and growing sector in both countries (200–250,000 full-time-equivalent employees in the mid-1980s in each country, and growing by some 12 per cent in the previous decade in each country); it does not use sophisticated machinery, and it provides substantial scope for the less-skilled type of employee. International differences in productivity might therefore not be expected to be large. Nevertheless, flowing from the training traditions embodied in renowned 'hotel schools' on the Continent, it is conceivable that higher productivity could arise from the way that work and responsibilities are organised there.

Two principal sources of variation needed to be eliminated in selecting matched samples of hotels for these comparisons: first, differences in hotels' coverage of restaurant and lodging activities and second, differences in the general standard and quality of service. The former was achieved by focusing the comparisons solely on lodging activities (bed and breakfast, excluding other restaurant and bar services), and counting only those employees – or the relevant fractions of their time – involved in those activities. The latter was achieved by confining the comparisons to hotels of the same 'quality grade'.

Rather than rely simply on the Institute's researchers' scale of values, the quality grades of the well-established Michelin guides was followed. These are based on anonymous inspectors' reports on a hotel's services judged as a whole. Hotels in both countries are classified into six grades, ranging from 'luxury in the traditional style' to 'simple comfort' (for Britain there is an additional lower grade of 'other recommended accommodation at moderate prices'). The same standards are used internationally in classifying hotels in these guides. Classifications provided by national tourist boards and automobile clubs (awarding 'stars' or 'crowns'), while no doubt valuable within each country, had the fundamental disadvantage for our purposes that they are usually not internationally comparable; more important, they are usually based on the mere provision – irrespective of quality – of specified facilities (lifts, full restaurant on the premises, number of public rooms, proportion of bedrooms with private bathrooms, telephones in rooms, and so on), rather than on a judgement on the establishment as a whole taking into account the efficiency and helpfulness of the staff and state of repair of the premises.

For this investigation hotels were chosen from those listed in the fourth and fifth grades from the top of the Michelin grading, designated as 'good average' and the (lower) 'fairly comfortable' grades (corresponding to the 'two gables' and 'one gable' symbols in the guides). Bearing in mind that the guides do not cover the very simplest of hotels, these grades probably span the national averages. The samples for each country were chosen equally from each of these two grades; the hotels were of medium size, with 20–100 bedrooms, and were all in large towns. Where a choice of hotels was listed for any town, preference was given to those in the middle of the price range within each grade. In reality, of course, the range of qualities is not a series of distinct grades but a continuum; and, not surprisingly, some variability in quality was found within each of the two grades that were visited. Nevertheless, nothing observed on the Institute's visits cast doubt on the international comparability of the average sampled hotel within each grade.

Taking guest-nights in each hotel as a measure of its output, and the number of full-time-equivalent employees as the input, it was found that German hotels employed 0.25 persons per guest-night, and the British 0.49. German hotels thus required just over half (51 per cent) of the labour per guest-night as did British hotels of the same quality grading – a very much greater difference than anticipated.[9]

Average bed-occupancy rates in the samples were similar, at 54 and 57 per cent in Britain and Germany respectively (close to the 56 per cent recorded in the available official statistics for both England as a whole and for Berlin in 1987).

In an attempt to trace the sources of the overall gap in productivity, two sub-categories of employees were distinguished: first, those engaged mainly in the more physical work of housekeeping, including housemaids, linen porters and housekeeping supervisors – a group for whom extensive systematic courses of vocational training might seem less necessary; and second, those engaged in the organisational work associated with reception – including preparation of bills, accepting payments, book-keeping, assisting guests in their varied requirements – for whom extensive vocational courses seem more obviously important. In both these sub-activities the German hotels showed substantially greater efficiency, requiring only 59 and 63 per cent respectively of the number of full-time-equivalent personnel per guest-night as the British hotels. Personnel engaged in managerial, maintenance and other activities, aside from housekeeping or reception, formed a somewhat lower proportion of the workforce in Germany than in Britain (29 as against 36 per cent); this accounts for the lower overall productivity ratio for Britain noted above in relation to total employment in the hotels visited.

To allow for differences between the two countries' sampled hotels in a number of ancillary factors, a fuller statistical analysis was undertaken; this took into account differences in the proportion of hotels that were of the *hôtel garni* type (that is, only breakfast was served, but there was no full restaurant on the premises), variations in hotel size, and whether the hotels were in the largest cities or in smaller towns. This analysis changed the results slightly, in that statistically significant differences were found between London and English provincial hotels (perhaps originating in the higher occupancy rates usual in London). On this fuller analysis, German hotels required 68 per cent of the employees in London hotels per guest-night, and a mere 46 per cent of the employees in English provincial hotels.[10]

A small parallel study of five Dutch hotels yielded personnel requirements per guest-night very similar to those found in Germany.

Surprising as it may seem, in short, the estimated gap in productivity between Britain and Germany (as well as between Britain and the Netherlands) in this branch of the service sector was quite as large as in manufacturing – perhaps even larger.

Machinery

The inter-country differences observed in the National Institute's matched samples of plants in respect of machinery and of workforce skills may next be considered as possible sources of the productivity differences described above; machinery differences are described in this section, and skills in the following section. These two factors should not, however, be regarded as independent: the types of machinery chosen by each firm, and the ways in which they are modified for its particular needs, often depend on the levels of skills that are already available. At the same time, skill-training is also usually modified in response to changed technological requirements; but the promptness and success of that response in training varies from one country to another depending, among other matters, on previous general educational and training levels.

In this section we shall need to refer to many aspects of machinery and equipment: degree of automation, ancillary feeding and off-loading devices, linkage of successive machines to avoid reloading, use of dedicated special-purpose machinery, the average age of machinery, its national origin, and rates of breakdown. The space available here permits no more than a selection of illustrations of the more significant contrasts observed between the countries (fuller details are to be found in the original reports).

Breakdown and maintenance

In retrospect it seems clear that inter-country differences in the ability to maintain complex machinery in efficient running order provide a key to many other differences that were observed. Problems of machinery maintenance in British industry are of long standing; for example, in 1975 the Prime Minister's 'Think Tank' (then known as the Central Policy Review Staff or CPRS) reported on car manufacture: 'despite the fact that British manufacturers employ 50–70 per cent more plant maintenance personnel than their Continental competitors, on identical equipment mechanical breakdowns result in the loss of twice as many production hours as on the Continent'.[11] The Institute's observations of matched samples of plants yielded broadly similar inferences. In factories producing kitchen cabinets, half of the British factories (five out of nine visited) exhibited severe malfunctioning on one of the main production lines at the time of the visit (in three factories, main lines were stopped and undergoing repair at the time of the visit; in two others, the lines were operating but their output required rectification). In none of the comparable German plants was a breakdown or serious malfunction observed on a main production line.[12]

Similarly in clothing production: in half the British plants visited one or more complex pieces of modern equipment (computerised marker-cutting, fusing machinery, bagging equipment) was not functioning correctly at the time of the visit; again, no breakdowns of this sort were observed in the comparable German sample.[13] In biscuit production, emergency downtime in the British sample of plants visited accounted for 10 per cent of planned machine working time, compared with an average of 5 per cent aimed at by the better British plants, and an actual average of 3–4 per cent in comparable samples visited in France, Germany and the Netherlands.[14] There thus seems to be a continuing British problem in maintaining the smooth running of machinery.[15]

Automatic feeding, off-loading and transfer

The type of machinery installed differed less among countries than did the ancillary devices attached to each machine for the purposes of: (a) automatically feeding materials or components in bulk into the machine, without the need for human intervention to feed each workpiece separately; (b) automatically off-loading into bins – without human handling– after that production stage has been completed; and (c) automatic transfer from one machine to the next, placing the component in the correct position on the next machine for the next operation. These ancillary devices are important features of modern technology, and are gradually replacing unskilled and semi-skilled operatives. They were more frequently observed in Continental than in British plants: for example, less automation was observed in British firms in feeding metal components (with the help of hoppers, strip-feeders) for presswork, and in the use of automatic turntables to present different faces of metalwork for polishing by rotary mops; similarly in woodworking, automated hoists for feeding cabinet panels for cutting and drilling were more frequent on the Continent.

The probabilities of failure cumulate if machines are linked; with a greater risk of breakdown in Britain on any individual machine or transfer device, it is not surprising that linkage of successive machines was less frequently undertaken in Britain. A foreman in one of the British factories explained: a defect in any one machine on a linked line would stop the whole line – whereas, if it is not part of a linked line, a broken-down machine can be bypassed using spare capacity.

Automated feeding devices require greater consistency in the materials they handle than does a human operator, who can often take steps to compensate for variations, say, in the 'temper' or stiffness of materials; such variations in materials may slow down a human operator but production will not completely cease, as it might with an automatic feeding device. Consistency in the quality of raw materials to be machined presented a greater problem in Britain than in Germany; there seemed less appreciation in British than in German metalworking firms of the value of paying a premium for higher-quality sheet steel (tighter dimensional tolerance, controlled burr on edges, and so on) in order to permit trouble-free running of automated lines.[16] Similar problems in the consistency of raw materials were also mentioned by British producers in other branches of industry. For example, in clothing production the degree of stretch of cloth in different directions during sewing or pressing needed to be subject to closer tolerances when garments are manufactured in bulk; and in biscuit production, the consistency of fats (moisture content, melting point) needed to be more closely monitored if automatic mixing were to operate successfully.

National origin of machinery

International specialisation in the production of machinery has grown rapidly in the past generation and, not surprisingly, machinery from many countries was observed in virtually all the sampled plants visited in the National Institute's enquiries. Few sectors of the British machine-tool industry seemed to have kept pace with international competition, however. The consequences were evident in the larger proportion of imported machinery seen on most British factory floors, and in the relatively small proportion of British machinery to be seen on Continental factory floors.

To quote some examples: virtually all woodworking machinery seen in the British sample of plants was imported (mainly from Germany or Italy); most computer-numerically-controlled (CNC) metalworking machinery in Britain was Japanese; all industrial sewing machines seen in Britain were imported (mainly from Japan, Germany, Italy: the huge Singer sewing machine plant in Britain ceased production in 1979). In contrast, German manufacturing firms, in all the industries examined, mainly used machinery produced by Germany's highly developed machine-tool industry, with only an admixture from specialist Italian, Swiss or Japanese machine producers. It was the view of manufacturers in all countries visited that the use of locally made machinery was an advantage in terms of availability of advice on specialist modifications and installation, and in the supply of spare parts. The burden that British manufacturers had to bear in consequence of their need to rely on imported machinery – because of the decline of the British machine-tool industry – appeared to have eased somewhat in the past decade with improvements in air transport for the supply of spare parts, and the simplification of import formalities; but the burden undoubtedly remained significant.

Food-processing machinery was one of the exceptions we observed where significant – though never predominant – numbers of British machines were observed in Continental factories.

Other equipment

Many differences were observed in smaller matters, such as layout of equipment and detailing of small tools and jigs; of these it is perhaps worth recording some simple details of the greater attention paid in German hotels to labour-saving design of equipment. Thus, furniture and washing facilities were more often flush with the floor, so that dust did not require to be removed from under them, or they were suspended from walls so that floor-cleaning beneath was easy; large fully-equipped 'chambermaid trolleys' were also used more widely in German hotels, leading to more systematic and efficient working routines.

Age of machinery and installation of CNC machinery

By and large there were no very important differences between countries in the average age of machinery installed in the Institute's matched samples of plants; if anything, British plants tended to have a slightly newer stock of machinery than their Continental counterparts. This is consistent with findings from previous postal surveys of installed machinery in a number of countries, carried out by machine-tool producers' associations; these indicated, for example, that in 1982 Britain's stock of metalworking machine tools was only twelve years old on average, compared with 14–15 years in France, Germany and the USA.[17]

Notwithstanding the slightly younger age of British machinery, it tended to be not as technically advanced as machinery on the Continent. For example, just under half the British sample of metalworking firms had installed some CNC machinery in 1983–4, whereas nearly all the matched German sample of firms had done so; in the Institute's subsequent comparison of British and Dutch engineering firms in 1990–91, CNC machinery accounted for 20 per cent of all major machines in British firms visited, but for 35 per cent of the comparable sample of Dutch firms.[18] Two reasons can be advanced for this difference. First, we have already noted that breakdown problems were more frequent in Britain: they were particularly frequent in new and complex machinery, including those with CNC controls. In Britain it thus made sense to delay the introduction of new, complex, automated machinery as long as possible, and wait till it is smoothly in operation elsewhere. This lag in introducing newer technology in Britain clearly manifested itself in lower relative productivity. Machinery suppliers interviewed by National Institute researchers (to supplement information gained from machinery users) confirmed that teething and subsequent heavy maintenance problems were significantly more prevalent among British than Continental users; British fitters' capabilities were sometimes so low that serious 'teething' problems had arisen simply because installation instructions had not been correctly followed.

Second, in considering reasons for the lower use of CNC machinery in Britain, it needs to be remembered that CNC machinery is economical only for a certain range of production runs: it is not easy to frame a general rule but, broadly speaking, CNC is appropriate where a variety of medium-sized batches – perhaps of 50–1,000 units each – is required, and the specifications of the different batches lie within the range of alternative facilities available on the CNC machining complex. Where only single items ('one offs'), or small unrelated batches, are to be produced, the cost of setting up is much the same whether traditional or modern CNC machinery is used; in such circumstances there is no point in bearing the higher overhead costs of CNC. At the other extreme, where very long runs are to be produced (using mass production methods), the flexibility of CNC machinery remains largely unused; it is then worth developing dedicated special-purpose machine lines, since they can be designed to work more rapidly on their specific tasks.[19]

The special virtue of modern CNC technology is that it enables a mix of smaller batches of 'made-to-measure' varieties to be produced to suit individual customers' requirements at much less extra cost than previously: that virtue was evidently better exploited on the Continent than in Britain. Britain, on the other hand, has tended to concentrate on improving the large-scale production of standardised varieties. While one must not overstate the extent of this simplified contrast, it provides a significant clue to underlying differences in national capabilities. That contrast was manifest in the production of kitchen furniture (where Britain mass-produced DIY standard kitchen cabinets, and the Germans produced made-to-measure rigid high-quality cabinets); in the production of ladies' outerwear (long runs of standard styles in Britain, small runs of more expensive fashion items in Germany); in the production of biscuits and, to some extent, also in engineering components.

Decisions as to the variety and types of products to be made thus affect the type of machinery installed and the ancillary feeding and automating mechanisms; that joint complex of decisions – that is, affecting both products and equipment – is related to supplies of skills, to which we next turn.

Skilled manpower and its deployment

That more vocational training to certified levels takes place in Continental Europe than in Britain is beyond dispute, as discussed in chapter 2 above with the help of national statistics of the qualifications of the current workforce and statistics of new qualifications awarded each year. Our task here is to focus on the workplace: we need to ask how those additional supplies of skills are distributed at typical Continental workplaces among various levels of technical complexity and responsibility; and whether there are evident signs that those additional skills contribute to higher productivity. This section attempts some answers on the basis of the matched samples of plants observed in the National Institute's international comparisons.

To avoid misunderstanding of the role of skill certification in Continental workplaces today, some general aspects need preliminary mention. First, the role of skill certification as a condition for employment: it is accepted in most countries that certification is essential in certain professional occupations – for example, medicine, law – before being permitted to practise. The complexities of such occupations are such that customers are not able (or cannot usually spare the time) to judge competence; the deleterious restrictive practices associated with certification (limited entry, high charges to the public) are usually judged to be outweighed by the benefits of public protection against charlatans. Similar certification requirements are applied to craft and technical occupations in most countries for occupations where public safety is at risk, for example, in certain categories of high-voltage electrical work, or work on high-pressure boilers.[20] Certification restrictions on the independent practice of a wider group of craft occupations are applied in certain countries; in Switzerland and Germany, for example, a car repair garage is required to be under the control of a qualified master craftsman (*Meister*) – that is, someone who has passed not only his craft-level examinations, but also a series of higher examinations taken usually after at least three years of employment in the trade, combined with further attendance at evening classes to help prepare for those examinations (a considerable list of independent *Handwerk* occupations fall into this category, such as building craftsmen, plumbers, TV repairers). These restrictions derive historically from the medieval guilds, and their continued justification today seems sensible in some occupations. In other occupations the public interest may be adequately safeguarded if uncertified persons who practise independently make it clear to customers that they lack formal qualifications.

It needs to be emphasised that formal qualification requirements do not apply on the Continent when it comes to employment, as distinct from setting up in business on one's own; a Continental firm may choose to employ whomever it regards as competent to carry out a job, irrespective of formal qualifications, much as an English employer is permitted to do. The only requirement is that a *Meister* must be employed if the firm is engaged in work that comes within regulated *Handwerk* trades. Consequently, within each category of occupation compared in the Institute's matched samples of plants, a mix of personnel with and without vocational qualifications was found in all countries; our comparisons therefore focused on the *proportions* of persons in each category of occupations who held relevant qualifications at equivalent levels.

A second preliminary matter is by way of a general caution in evaluating international skill comparisons. The comparisons carried out by the Institute, and the judgements based on them on the contribution of skill training to productivity, can relate only to the qualification systems *taken as a whole*. For particular occupations in some countries there may seem to be too many trainees, or training may seem unnecessarily long (too many qualified bakers in Germany is a frequently quoted example); such situations may have arisen because of lags in adapting the training system to shifts in demand, or for reasons of social equity and administrative feasibility. It is thus entirely possible that *particular* manufacturing operations are carried out in one country by an unqualified group of operatives as efficiently as in another country by a more highly qualified group; but overall efficiency may be greater in the latter country because of the way the training system works as a whole. Even those working on simple operations often benefit from what may seem to be unnecessarily extended training since they are more flexible between jobs, and are more adaptable when it comes to adapting to technical changes. In other words (and at the risk of labouring a point – but one that has frequently been misunderstood), however precise we may attempt to be here in comparing percentages of qualified personnel in particular occupations in different countries, such comparisons should be taken as no more than providing broad guidance on moves towards attaining higher productivity in the economy as a whole, and not as providing unambiguous quantitative targets for specific occupations or specific firms.

Let us now survey international skill differences in the various industries compared, distinguishing four broad occupational groups according to level and type of skill: (a) occupations involving mainly routine work requiring little technical skill or judgement (at best – speed and stamina), such as machine loader, packer, chambermaid; (b) moderately skilled work, requiring a degree of judgement and precision, such as maintenance mechanic, or sewing machinist; (c) skilled occupations, such as those concerned with machinery maintenance and technical support; (d) foremen and supervisors, requiring a mix of technical and organisational capabilities.

Routine work

Personnel engaged in simple routine manufacturing tasks – loading components for metalworking machinery, packaging of biscuits, hotel chambermaids – were not usually required to have vocational qualifications in any of the countries, and usually had none. At this basic level there were no great differences between Britain and the Continent.

Increasing preference for the precision of basic vocational qualifications for new staff were nevertheless expressed where automation was increasing. For example, in metalworking plants a single person now often loads a group of automated machines, keeps an eye on their correct working, and maintains written records of output; similar developments affect other occupations which were previously routine and unskilled. Young recruits for this kind of work in the Netherlands are now expected to have attained a satisfactory certificate from a vocational secondary school (LBO grade B or C). Such preferences were not voiced in Britain, probably because there are no comparable vocational secondary schools with relevant school-leaving certificates.

Moderately skilled work

The more complex the work, the greater was the gap observed between Britain and the Continent in the proportions of the workforce with vocational qualifications. The gap was not as great in engineering as in other industries, since there has been a long history of engineering apprenticeships in Britain – even if it was never as quantitatively nor qualitatively developed as on the Continent. Thus, among turners and millers in the Institute's Dutch sample of engineering plants, some 80 per cent had attained craft qualifications: while in the matched British engineering sample some 40 per cent had attained that level. In modern woodworking (kitchen cabinet) plants – a sector which is mainly outside older engineering traditions – some 90 per cent of those engaged in shop-floor production had attained craft-level qualifications in the German sample, compared with a mere 10 per cent in the British sample. Perhaps even more remarkable was the contrast in plants manufacturing women's outerwear in the qualifications of sewing machinists: some 80 per cent of German machinists had acquired examined vocational qualifications, following a systematic traineeship at work combined with part-time college courses lasting at least two years, whereas in the matched British sample not a single machinist had attained a vocational qualification at a similar level (Part II of the City and Guilds course).

The production consequences were evident in engineering in the greater general ability of Continental firms to meet customers' specialised needs, and thus make confident plans for expansion despite increased international competition; this contrasted with declining employment and worries about survival expressed by many of the British engineering firms in our sample. Similarly, in woodworking, higher skills have led to the well-known higher quality of German fitted kitchens (precision, finish) as mentioned in the opening section of this chapter; and the same is true of the higher quality-bracket targeted by German clothing manufacturers.

Looking at production processes in more detail, clothing firms – surprising as it may seem – probably provided the clearest examples of how training directly improved productivity. First, at the end of most lines of sewing machinists observed in Britain, someone was usually engaged in 'unpicking' faulty work – while this was never observed on visits to the matched German sample (not that faulty stitching never occurred in German plants, but it must have been sufficiently less frequent to yield such an evident contrast). Second, a little more complex and more important: when putting a new style into production, an average of 2–3 days 'running-in' to reach full operating speed was required by German machinists, whereas the average British machinist required several weeks to reach full production speed. In that 'running-in' period German machinists were able to work directly from technical sketches, with only the occasional need for advice from their supervisor on difficult points; while in British plants very few machinists could work directly from technical sketches, and required their supervisors physically to demonstrate new operations. British plants thus understandably opted for the production of longer runs – with fewer changeovers – and for less elaborately stitched products; even so, two and a half times as many checkers ('passers') and supervisors were required per machinist in British than in Continental clothing plants (one for every twelve machinists in Germany, one for every five in Britain).[21]

Maintenance and technician teams

To understand the sources of the higher rate of breakdown of British machinery, and of the better adaptation of Continental machinery to a plant's particular products, it is necessary to remember that there is very often a difference between someone called a 'skilled craftsman' in British industry and a qualified *Fachmann* in German industry (or those with corresponding qualifications in other Continental countries). Staff on maintenance and technical support teams in Britain are described as 'skilled' usually on the basis of a time-served apprenticeship, sometimes combined with some form of participation in related courses within the framework of City and Guilds, but not necessarily having passed the relevant examinations. The foreman of the team has usually acquired formal qualifications with passes at City and Guilds examinations at Part II (or even Part III); but of other members of the team, it was often said that they 'attended some classes, but did not bother with examinations'. On the Continent, formal examinations and qualifications to craft level are usually the minimum for members of maintenance teams, and some – almost invariably including the foreman – have attained higher qualifications at technician or *Meister* level.

The differences observed between British and Continental maintenance and technical support teams in the proportions of employees with various levels of qualifications varied considerably according to the type of activities covered; the following comparisons illustrate the range of contrasts observed. In routine maintenance operations in British engineering plants, almost all team members were 'skilled' (as described above, mostly only time-served, but with some 'dilutees' to whom simpler tasks were delegated), whereas in the matched Dutch engineering sample all had acquired formal craft-level qualifications and – probably even more significant – half had also acquired higher diplomas at the equivalent of technician level (close to our Higher National Diplomas). In the same engineering samples, among technical support staff – concerned with production planning, quality control and R & D – the contrast was in the same direction, but at higher levels of qualification: in British plants some 45 per cent had attained technician or higher qualifications, while 80 per cent had attained such levels in the Dutch plants.[22] A more extreme contrast in maintenance teams was observed in clothing manufacturing, where machinery today includes not only complex industrial sewing machines but also advanced patterning and cutting equipment (as mentioned, the latter are now often computer-controlled): in the German clothing firms all mechanics had passed engineering apprenticeship examinations, while none had done so in the matched British clothing firms.

The difference between Britain and the Continent at this level seems to manifest itself in terms of practical outcomes in this way: someone who has followed a purely on-the-job route to learning a trade may be as competent in carrying out specified routine maintenance tasks as someone who has also attended college courses on theoretical aspects and passed written examinations. But, in the modern more technically complex world, it seems he or she is less likely to be competent in knowing – sufficiently precisely and sufficiently quickly – what may have gone wrong, or is likely to go wrong, which is the best way of putting it right, and be able to do so in a way that ensures it will not soon go wrong again. This is probably the source of the 'dearth of diagnostic skills' which has become a standard bleat in British industry.

Differences in the extent of preventive maintenance between Britain and the Continent must to a large extent be attributable to these differences in the skill levels of maintenance teams – though inadequate technical skills at intermediate management level must bear a share of the blame. Almost all Continental plants carried out routine programmes of preventive maintenance, whereas hardly any British plants did so; the consequences were apparent in the significantly lower rates of emergency breakdowns on the Continent described above. British practical engineering philosophy was close to the well-known simple view – 'if it ain't broke, don't fix it'; that is not an irrational policy if the requisite skills are sufficiently scarce (the Clapham rail disaster occurred not because the signal wiring was old and needed replacing, but because it had been replaced in the previous week, and replaced incompetently).[23]

Foremen and supervisors

Should those working at supervisory level – whether as foremen or at other intermediate levels of management – be chosen primarily because of their superior technical competence, or because of their superior general managerial skills? The scarcity of technical skills at intermediate management levels had made this into a question frequently debated in Britain.

The great number trained to *Meister* level in Germany has ensured that it is not an issue in that country. Roughly one in ten of all qualifying as craftsmen proceed, after a minimum of three years full-time practical experience, to advanced courses leading to *Meister* examinations; the courses include technical topics (more advanced than craftsman level) together with courses on management techniques and training methods. In large firms it is not unusual to find two or three craftsmen working as members of maintenance or technical teams who – in addition to their craft qualifications – - are taking, or have already passed, their *Meister* examinations, and are ready to submit themselves for a vacancy as foreman (or assistant manager, and so on) when it arises.

Our matched samples of firms reflected these differences. In the British metalworking sample, 85 per cent of production foremen (not maintenance foremen, discussed above) had acquired their positions solely on the basis of their working experience without any paper qualifications; only a small minority had even served an apprenticeship. In the matched German metalworking sample the situation was quite different: 80 per cent of foremen had acquired the qualification of *Meister*, and the remainder were taking courses towards that qualification (all had previously acquired formal craft qualifications). At the level of production controller in kitchen-cabinets plants – a complex organisational task requiring the grouping of similar orders for economy of production while meeting required delivery dates – hardly anyone engaged in this work in the British sample had any vocational qualification, while in the corresponding German sample this work was carried out by those with *Meister* qualifications.[24]

Similar contrasts between Britain and Germany were observed in the matched samples of clothing plants and of biscuit plants. The Dutch and French matched biscuit-producing plants presented contrasts with Britain similar to those shown by the German sample, but not quite as marked.

In hotel work the contrast in qualified staff at the supervisory level cast a particularly clear light on productivity consequences. As mentioned, neither British nor German hotels required vocational qualifications at the operative level – the chambermaid. The contrast in qualifications arose at the first supervisory level, known as the 'housekeeper': three-quarters of all housekeepers in the German sample of hotels had attained craft-level qualifications, following a standard three-year apprenticeship course (for *Hotelfachmann or -frau*) covering the full range of hotel functions; in the British sample not a single housekeeper had attended any external courses in hotel work.[25] The consequences were apparent in the greater proportion of organisational responsibility undertaken by the German housekeeper, who spent more time (in comparison with the British hotel housekeeper) on work-scheduling, stock control, purchasing, organising external services (laundry), and selecting labour-saving equipment. Efficient work-scheduling, we judged, was probably the single most important element in raising workforce productivity in German hotels.[26] In British hotels this range of routine organisational work was usually carried out at a higher level, by the manager; British managers consequently had less time than their German counterparts for longer-term matters, such as marketing campaigns, advance block-sales to tourist agencies and wholesalers, and the installation and improvement of computerised booking, invoicing, and other management aids.

Changing priorities

Forty years ago, in the early postwar period, an Anglo-American Productivity Council was established to find clues on how to raise industrial productivity in Britain. About fifty teams from Britain, each consisting of approximately a dozen industrialists, were sent to visit plants in their own industries in the United States; they returned after about a month's tour with many detailed examples of the application of American ingenuity to save labour and thus raise productivity.[27] The plants visited were mostly very large plants with over a thousand employees; plants of that size accounted for less than a third of industrial employment and, as one of the reports warned, 'were not necessarily representative of the whole of industry in the US'.[28] American industrial success at that time was based on a greater specialisation by each plant in more limited sections of the product range than usual in Britain; products were made on a much larger scale than in Britain, and by *less*-skilled labour. As the Pressed Metal team put it: 'the participation of skilled workers in American press plants [was] less than in Britain'.[29] Skilled work in America was broken down, on Taylorist principles, into constituent 'machine operations which can be performed by unskilled or semi-skilled workers'; 'the skills that [the operative] acquired were in his own limited operations, with little wider knowledge of his trade'.[30]

Some in Britain may still think that this is the correct route to improving Britain's industrial success; but, as has become clear from the comparisons with Continental Europe surveyed in the present chapter, technology has changed significantly since those days. Success today depends on replacing unskilled repetitive operations by automated machines, and on raising skill levels, so that a greater proportion of industrial personnel are capable of supervising, controlling, and resetting such machinery. The new objective is to produce a greater range of specialised variants to meet the needs of individual customers ('flexible specialisation'), and to do so with modern machinery on which small batches of variants do not incur heavy surcharges. Success depends on greater skills in choosing the right machinery, in modifying it so that it operates efficiently for the specialised products of that firm, and in maintaining it in good working order.

Government subsidies and tax incentives to encourage the purchase of more new machinery (accelerated depreciation for tax purposes) – however much they have been welcomed by industry – have not gone to the root of Britain's problem; and they are even less likely to do so in the modern technological world. Attention must rather be given to the incentives to acquire technical skills, and to the provision of better basic school-leaving standards – so that the average school-leaver does not regard the acquisition of high technological skills as presenting an insuperable intellectual challenge. The nature of the improvements required in basic schooling is the subject to which we turn in the next chapter.

4 Education and productivity

Britain's educational problem in international perspective

The need to raise Britain's educational standards is now more widely appreciated than even only a decade ago – and as much by the public at large as by policymakers. If education has not quite 'risen to the top of the political agenda' (as sometimes said), it has recently often appeared very near the top. International comparisons, whether of the high technical quality of imported manufactured goods or of schooling systems in other countries, have come prominently into the public eye; and they have increasingly raised doubts as to whether Britain's schooling system provides an adequate foundation for the workforce skills required in a modern technological world.

The task of this chapter is to examine with a degree of international perspective the underlying facts and figures relating to two aspects of Britain's schooling that bear on the economic efficiency of its workforce: standards attained at school in mathematics and in practical subjects (such as metalwork or technical drawing). Schooling attainments in these subjects form important parts of the bridges linking schooling, training and work. By limiting ourselves here to aspects of schooling bearing on economic efficiency, and examining them in some detail, we may hope to reach conclusions less subject to controversy than often in educational discussions, and to do so within the space of a single chapter. Comparisons of these particular subjects also provide wider insights into schooling effectiveness, in that adequate mathematical instruction is a prerequisite for progress in many parts of science; and the degree of specialisation in practical subjects in the final years of compulsory schooling bears on many pupils' subsequent readiness to undertake vocational education, and on their general motivation in those final years at school. The next two sections will thus deal, in turn, with mathematics and practical subjects; a final section discusses organisational aspects of schooling – differing between Britain and the Continent – that bear on pupils' attainments.

As explained in previous chapters, the advantage in workforce qualifications of Germany and other Continental countries lies hardly at all at the university graduate level (Britain now matches Germany in the proportion of graduates employed in manufacturing industry as a whole, and even slightly exceeds Germany's proportion in some industrial branches): rather, the advantage of those countries lies very substantially in attainments at the level of intermediate vocational qualifications – mainly of those who, when at school, were in the middle and lower ranges of school-attainment levels. To re-state the main point briefly: in round numbers close to 60 per cent in Germany, compared with some 30 per cent in Britain, attain vocational qualifications at craft level (broadly corresponding to City and Guilds Part II). To reach those vocational standards – say, at age nineteen to twenty – certain standards of general education need to be attained during the period of compulsory schooling, that is before fifteen or sixteen. If 'reading, writing and arithmetic' have not been sufficiently mastered by that age it becomes difficult, both for apprentices and for their teachers, to make satisfactory progress in colleges of further and vocational education. Our focus in this chapter thus needs to be not, as in many previous comparisons of education, on the achievements of prize British pupils in international educational Olympiads, but on standards reached by average and below-average pupils towards the end of compulsory schooling.

Mathematics

The need for a widespread competence in mathematics requires little elaboration: it is needed at a *basic* level by almost everyone when going shopping; at an *intermediate* level by craftsmen who have to calculate the volume of raw materials or the size of electrical flows, or in business transactions when calculating hire-purchase terms; and it is often needed at an *advanced* level in scientific work. Much teaching of science even at secondary schools hinges on basic algebraic manipulation (for example, the ability to transform simple equations in Newton's laws of motion and Ohm's law). Mathematics is a subject in which the average British pupil has for long been known to fall distinctly behind in international comparisons; and British employers, in listing their complaints about school-leaving standards, have repeatedly found it necessary to include poor mathematical attainments.

International tests

The most recent large-sample international comparisons of pupils' attainments in mathematics were carried out in 1991; but the essential features of (what we may call) the 'British problem in mathematics' became evident in quantitative terms in the first major international comparison carried out in 1963–4. It is as well to begin there. That first *International Study of Achievements in Mathematics* was carried out in a dozen countries; seventy internationally agreed questions were set to about 3,000 pupils in each country at age thirteen – the latest age when pupils in virtually all the countries concerned were in compulsory full-time education (additional tests were set to pupils in their pre-university year, aged eighteen to nineteen, but the findings are not immediately relevant here: only a small fraction of top-attainers are at school at that age, and that fraction varies substantially from country to country). The study was carried out by an international academic group known as the International Association for the Evaluation of Educational Achievement (known as IEA for short).[1] The ostensible object of these studies was to compare the factors in different countries that contribute to successful learning; for example, how class size and time devoted to this subject at school (or in homework) are related to high scores within each country. There was less ostensible concern among the sponsors of these studies with ranking countries by average attainments; nevertheless, when these and related studies are taken together, important inferences can be drawn as to the nature of Britain's educational problem.

The distribution of test scores in mathematics for all 13 year-olds in England in that first international study is summarised here in table 4.1 in comparison with France, Germany, the Netherlands, Japan and the United States. If we define low-attainers as those with a score of 5 or under out of a maximum score of 70, as many as 24 per cent of all pupils in England were found in that category, compared with only 8–10 per cent in Germany, the Netherlands and Japan, and 14 per cent in France. None of the other countries in that enquiry had as high a proportion of low-attainers as England, though the United States (on which more will be said in a moment) came close to England. Roughly speaking, we may say that there were 2–3 times as many low-attainers in England as in our leading European industrial competitors.

We can examine the gap for low-attainers more directly from that IEA inquiry by comparing the scores of English pupils in Secondary Modern schools with the scores of German pupils in *Hauptschulen*; these schools catered for pupils who were broadly in the lower section of the academic attainment range in each country. Average scores of 12.9 were recorded

Table 4.1 *Summary distribution of scores in international mathematical tests of 13-year-old pupils, England compared with five other countries 1963–4*

Score(a)	England	France	Germany(b)	Netherlands	Japan	USA
<5	24	14	8	10	8	22
6-30	49	68	59	57	38	62
31-51	22	16	30	25	40	14
>51	5	2	3	8	14	1
	100	100	100	100	100	100
Average score	19	18	25	24	31	16
CV(%)(c)	88	68	53	67	54	82

Source: From the IEA study (see p. 126, note 15), vol. II, p. 22 ('population 1a' *all* 13-year-olds; totals may not sum to 100 because of rounding).
Notes:
(a) Out of maximum 70.
(b) Approximate: estimated from original tabulation as follows. Germany participated only on the basis of classes containing *most* 13-year-olds ('population 1b', not 'population 1a'). That is, the German figures as originally published omitted the very highest attainers of that age who had 'skipped a class' and were now in a higher class, and also omitted the very lowest attainers of that age who had 're-peated' a year and were now in a lower class. For convenience of exposition here we have adjusted the original published figures for Germany by reference to the differences between the alternative bases reported for neighbouring countries with similar policies on class-repeating: France, the Netherlands and Belgium. The adjustment was important only for the lowest category of pupils (a score of under 5), who would have been shown as accounting for only 4 per cent of all German pupils instead of the estimated 8 per cent as shown above.
(c) Coefficient of variation (standard deviation divided by average, derived from original source).

for Secondary Modern pupils in England, and 22.4 for *Hauptschule* pupils in Germany: an astonishing gap![2] On the basis of IEA tests administered at that time to parallel groups of pupils who were a year younger, it appears that a one-year difference in ages was associated with an average gain of some 4.4 points by Secondary Modern pupils; subject to obvious qualifications, the difference between the English and German average scores (in this lower section of the attainment range) can thus be said to be equivalent to an English lag behind Germany of just over two years of English schooling. Yet another way of expressing the contrast is to note that the German average score of 22.4 by pupils in the least-academic stream of schools (those catering for the *lower portion* of the academic ability range) was slightly above the average score by *all* English pupils of 20.1; very broadly speaking, the German system had raised the attainment of its lowest half of pupils to that of the average of all pupils in England.[3]

On the other hand, for pupils in the top attainment-range shown in table 4.2 (p.82), those scoring over 50 out of a maximum of 70 points, England's 5 per cent of pupils in that category compared favourably with France and Germany's mere 2 per cent; nor were English top pupils too far below the 8 per cent of the Netherlands, though even then they were substantially below Japan's 14 per cent.

England thus had an unusually large share of low-attainers, combined with a respectably large share of high-attainers. In terms of the coefficient of variation (final row of table 4.2), pupils in England had a 60 per cent higher variability in attainments than pupils in Germany and Japan, and a 30 per cent higher variability than France and the Netherlands. Such wide differences in variability deserve as much attention as differences in *average* scores to which attention is usually directed. In the calculation of average scores the relatively good performance of English high-attaining pupils partly offsets, and hides, the relatively poor performance of England's low-attainers. A related general point was made some twenty years ago by the American educationist Professor Benjamin Bloom, one of the main motivators of these international studies: 'across the world, differences in attainments by the bottom 90 per cent [of pupils are much greater] than among the top 5 per cent'.[4] His remark has greater weight today because of the technological developments that continue to depress the relative demand for those with low schooling attainments.

Because of its economic pre-eminence, the United States must be mentioned here, but its educational system suffers from serious problems and we shall not need to look at it in great detail. Considered as a whole, the success of its educational system relies on providing the median pupils with full-time schooling until nineteen, compared with under seventeen in Britain and Germany. It is thus a highly expensive system. Attainments at secondary school in the USA, however, develop slowly. In terms of the proportion of low-attaining pupils, the USA came second from the bottom in the international study just quoted – that is, only just above England – with 22 per cent of its pupils in that category compared with England's 24 per cent (and 8 per cent in Germany and Japan). In addition, the United States was at a disadvantage in having fewer high attainers than in England (for example, only 1.4 per cent of US pupils, compared with 5 per cent of English pupils, attained a score of over 50). The *average* score for all US pupils in that survey consequently came out lower than England, even though the USA did not have quite as many low-attainers.

The educational basis for the economic success of that great country thus clearly does not rest on high attainments at secondary school; on the contrary, deficiencies at that level of schooling – and particularly of pupils on non-academic school tracks – are now of as much public concern there as they are in Britain. Unemployment among the young and unskilled is a serious problem there; and average earnings per hour, far from rising as a result of technical advances, have slightly declined in real terms over the past twenty years, and more so for those who are unqualified. Methods of schooling in Continental Europe and Japan are now looked on in the United States as sources of inspiration for improving US school-leaving standards; from the point of view of our concerns here, the USA is thus to be considered more as a country suffering from similar educational problems to those of Britain, rather than providing any exemplary message which may be of immediate help.[5]

International surveys of pupils' attainments were subsequently extended by the IEA to other subjects. Tests of science attainments by 14-year-olds were carried out in 1970. The results again pointed to English pupils' low average scores and greater variability: the coefficient of variation of English scores was 25–30 per cent greater than in Sweden, the USA, Hungary and Japan. Scores attained by the lowest tenth of pupils in Germany were attained by the lowest quarter of pupils in England. In science, as for mathematics mentioned above, it thus appears that England had 2–3 times as many low-attainers as Germany.[6]

Tests of reading comprehension by 14-year-olds were carried out by the IEA in 1970; they again showed higher variability in England as compared with three other countries for which that analysis was carried out – Sweden, the USA, and Hungary – with the lower quartile of pupils appearing particularly low.[7]

Scotland is often thought to have a schooling system superior to England's. This seems to be modestly supported by the IEA tests for reading; but, surprising as it may seem, Scottish pupils' attainment in mathematics and science were almost indistinguishable from England's in respect of low averages and high variability of scores.

Let us now return to mathematics and look at more recent results. The IEA carried out a second survey of mathematical attainments in 1981, seventeen years after its first study of that subject; in that intervening period English secondary schooling had been substantially transformed from a selective to a comprehensive system. Some twenty countries took part in this second study (compared with a dozen in the first), including a number of developing countries. Japan again came top with an average score of 62 per cent, followed by the Netherlands (57), Hungary (56), France (53) and Belgium (52); Germany did not participate in this round. England's average score of 47 per cent was distinctly lower but, as in the first survey, was slightly above Sweden (42) and the USA (45).[8]

On the basis of similar tests administered to parallel groups of pupils who were a year younger than the main sample (as in the previous comparisons with Germany mentioned above), it may be said that average Japanese pupils were nearly two years ahead of average English pupils in 1981: there had been negligible change in the advantage of Japanese pupils, on this measure, since the IEA study of 1964.[9] Taking an average of the scores of the Netherlands, France and Belgium to represent Western Europe, England could be said to lag by about a year's schooling behind this Western European group, and probably more if biases in England's poor response rate could be taken into account. It should also be remembered that formal schooling starts a year later in these Western European countries than in Britain – at age six rather than five – so that at least two years of progress are 'lost' under the British schooling system. France's series of initiatives in that period to raise educational attainments seemed to have borne fruit since its average score in the 1981 tests was much the same as for the Netherlands and Belgium, whereas in 1964 France had been distinctly lower.

The variability of mathematical attainments by pupils in 1981 can be judged on the basis of thirty-seven so-called 'anchor-item' questions that were set identically both in 1964 and in 1981.[10] For English pupils, a small reduction in variability occurred between 1964 and 1981, of about a tenth as measured by the coefficient of variation. However, compared with other countries the variability of English pupils' attainments remained high, at some 50 per cent above France and Japan, and considerably higher than Sweden and Hungary; but it was now slightly exceeded by the USA.

The 'anchor-item' questions included a greater share of basic mathematical topics; a not untypical question was:

> On level ground a boy 5 units tall casts a shadow 3 units long.
> At the same time, a nearby telephone pole 45 units high casts
> a shadow – what is the length of that shadow?

In the survey of 1964 that question had been answered correctly by 56 per cent of English pupils; by 1981 it was answered correctly by only 29 per cent of English pupils (compared with 61 per cent of Japanese pupils).[11] That is to say, in broad terms, this question could be answered correctly in England in 1981 by hardly more than that proportion of pupils who had previously been in the grammar school stream.

On all the anchor questions, English pupils in 1981 were able to answer correctly only some 30 per cent (adjusted for guessing), which is close to the example just considered. Only in one of the thirty-seven anchor questions did English pupils fare better in 1981 than in 1964; in six questions there was no statistically significant difference between these two years; but *in twenty-nine out of the same thirty-seven questions English pupils in 1981 did significantly worse than in 1964.*[12] Grouping these anchor questions into arithmetic, algebra, geometry and statistics, England was the only country which showed declines in average scores for all four groups.[13]

This is a remarkable record of decline. Even after allowing for a slight difference in average ages of pupils in the two surveys (they were about three months younger in the later survey) it appears, from a calculation based on attainments of pupils of different ages, that the fall in scores in the period 1964–81 was equivalent to a loss of some eleven months of learning.[14] In other words, in basic mathematical topics, pupils aged fourteen in 1981 were on average only at the level that 13-year-olds had reached in 1964.

There is little doubt that most countries in the past generation have shifted their mathematical curricula to varying extents away from traditional – especially arithmetical – topics, partly because of the increasing availability of cheap calculators, and partly because the 'modern mathematics' movement led to the inclusion of a series of new topics. It goes without saying that if there is to be progress in the curriculum as a result of the inclusion of new topics, it would not be surprising to find less time devoted to older topics, accompanied by a decline in pupils' attainments in those topics. Judging from this comparison of the 1964 and 1981 international tests, it seems that changes in that period – whether in curricula, examination systems, school organisation or other matters (teacher training?) – were less successful in Britain than in other countries, and did not bear any obvious fruit when measured on internationally agreed tests.

In 1990 there was a further round of international tests of mathematical attainments of pupils aged thirteen. The tests were carried out by a US agency (the Educational Testing Service of Princeton, N.J., which had much experience of testing within the USA), and were sponsored by the US government because of its increased concern with low schooling standards there; the tests were named the International Assessment of Educational Progress (IAEP, not to be confused with the IEA which was the body responsible for the previous studies). Some twenty countries participated; summary results are shown in table 4.2 for England and four other countries. Within Europe, Switzerland's average score was highest at 71 per cent correct, followed by Hungary (68), France (64), Italy (64) and then Eng-

Table 4.2 *Scores in international mathematics tests of 13-year-old pupils (averages and extreme deciles), England compared with four other countries, 1990*

	England	France	Italy(c)	Switzerland	USA
Arithmetic average	59.5(a)	64.2	64.0	70.8	55.3
Highest decile	89.3	89.3	88.0	93.3	82.7
Lowest decile	32.0(a)	37.3	36.5	50.7	29.3
Relative variability (%)(b)	95	81	81	60	97

Source: IAEP Study, 1990; extracted from Lapointe *et al.*, *Learning Mathematics*, p. 145.
Notes:
(a) Adjusted for low response (see p. 129, note 37).
(b) Difference betweeen highest and lowest decile as percentage of arithmetic mean.
(c) Emilia-Romagna only (sample response rate satisfactory at 78 per cent).

land at 60 per cent; the US average score was only 55 per cent. This was the first time Switzerland had participated in such international comparisons. The Netherlands, which was the top-attaining European country in the 1981 IEA study, did not participate; nor did Germany. On a broad view we may, however, regard Germany, the Netherlands and Switzerland as pursuing teaching approaches with considerable elements of similarity (predominantly whole-class teaching, emphasis on mastery of basics); it may be adequate for our purposes here to regard each of those countries as representative of that Western European group. Japan also did not participate; but two Asian countries following educational approaches similar to Japan's did – Korea and Taiwan; their average scores, both at 73 per cent, were slightly ahead of Switzerland's 71 per cent.

Switzerland's performance was also very remarkable in that its lowest tenth of pupils scored distinctly higher than the lowest tenth in any other country.[15] A full third of English pupils were able to reach no more than the score of the Swiss lowest tenth.[16] In other words, there were some three times as many low achievers in mathematics in England as in Switzerland, measured against the same international criterion; this is similar to the ratio noted in the 1964 comparison between Germany and England. Switzerland's success with 'low-attainers' as recorded in this IAEP survey fully concurred with observations by our teams of school inspectors and teachers on visiting Swiss schools in 1992–4. At the top end of the attainment-range, the IAEP survey suggests that England in 1990 no longer displayed the advantage over other countries that had appeared in the 1964 tests (see table 4.2, row 2). US attainments at this age remained slightly weaker than Britain's.

Variability of pupils' attainments built into the National Curriculum

The variability of English pupils' attainments in mathematics was given prominence in the 1982 official inquiry by the Cockcroft Committee into the teaching of school mathematics in England and Wales. 'A seven year difference' in pupils' attainments at age eleven was identified by the Committee in its report, *Mathematics Counts*, and has subsequently been widely quoted; that is to say, a typical cross-section of pupils aged eleven might be expected to contain pupils ranging in attainments from those of average pupils aged seven to those of average pupils aged fourteen.[17]

The extent of variability in attainments of pupils of a given age is an important issue; it determines the optimum organisation of classes and the choice of teaching methods. Three reservations must, however, be attached to the bold summary statement in the report of the Cockcroft Committee. First, we need to be clear as to the *proportion* of pupils having attainments within that seven-year span: the range spanned, for example, by 80 per cent of pupils may be expected to be only about half that spanned by 99 per cent of pupils (it would be almost exactly a half if attainments followed a statistically normal distribution). Any stated span is thus arbitrary unless the proportion of pupils covered is stated. Nothing was said explicitly by the Cockcroft Committee; but specimen test questions quoted in their report suggest that the middle 70 per cent of pupils might have been in the Cockcroft Committee's mind when speaking of a 'seven year difference'. A second reservation is that the empirical evidence produced was based, not on the results of a broad range of mathematical tests, but on just two or three specimen questions.[18] These were adequate to confirm that pupils' attainments at a given age vary; but they were inadequate in relation to the precision conveyed in mentioning 'seven years' as a measure of variability. Third, there was no recognition that the variability of pupils' attainments might be substantially lower in other countries, nor that the organisation of schooling might have a bearing on the variability of pupils' attainments. In short, the seven-year difference was put forward as something close to an established fact of nature – as immutable for practical purposes as, say, the 8cm standard deviation of adult men's heights in Britain – but without scientific foundation.

This 'stylised fact' subsequently had fundamental consequences for the organisation of the whole spectrum of curriculum subjects in British schools.

When the National Curriculum (NC) framework was prescribed under legislation at the end of the 1980s, levels of attainment were set down for each subject corresponding, first, to the *average* pupil at each age; second, the expected *variability* of attainments at each age was officially indicated in graphical form as 'a rough speculation about the limits within which about 80 per cent of pupils may be found to lie' (note 80, and not 70, per cent of pupils as might be inferred from the Cockcroft report).[19] This was intended to guide the breadth of levels of study to be provided for pupils in each age group. That graph (the 'TGAT graph', named after the NC Task Group on Assessment and Testing) indicated that at age eleven, 80 per cent of pupils were expected to have attainments lying between those of average pupils aged eight to fourteen; that is, a six-year span was then posited for the central 80 per cent of pupils.[20]

Whatever reasoning lay behind all this, Britain is now in the remarkable position of having incorporated – as part of its scheme for a National Curriculum in all subjects – a specified degree of variability in attainments for pupils within each age-group. As we have seen, the variability of English pupils' attainments is unusually wide by international standards – which is another way of saying that we have an unusually long tail of low achievers. An unfortunate accompaniment of the present approach is that no explicit target for a reduction in that variability has been put on to the political agenda; nevertheless, scores from tests set to all pupils (the controversial Standard Assessment Tasks – SATs) as part of the National Curriculum arrangements are now being used to identify weak schools for investigation by the inspectorate. That process can only be beneficial.

Weakness in arithmetic

The international surveys of pupils' mathematical attainments, referred to above, have also been helpful in identifying that the weakness of English pupils is particularly severe in one branch of that subject – arithmetic. Within arithmetic, three sub-branches were distinguished by the IAEP study of 13-year-old pupils in 1990: basic concepts (for example, what is a decimal number?); problem-solving (does the pupil know which technique to apply to a problem in an applied context?); and procedural knowledge (can the pupil actually subtract or multiply?). It is in this last sub-branch – procedural knowledge – that British pupils were most lacking. Two examples may be quoted. A subtraction sum with one decimal place $(21.2 - 3.4)$ was answered correctly by 85 per cent of pupils in Korea and Taiwan, by 80 per cent of pupils in France, Italy and Switzerland – but by only 49 per cent in England and Wales.[21]

Multiplication was more difficult: 9.2 × 2.5 was calculated correctly by 70 per cent of pupils in Korea and Taiwan, by 55 per cent in France, Italy and Switzerland – but by a mere 13 per cent of English pupils: fewer than in any of the twenty participating countries.[22]

These examples show how *average* English pupils compare in arithmetic with average pupils in other countries in the most recent international tests. To delineate how English pupils in the lower half of the academic attainment range compare internationally in specific arithmetical topics is more difficult, since the systematic international surveys considered so far have not been published in relevant detail. Some illustrative comparisons can, however, be drawn: in one of the German *Länder*, Baden-Württemberg (main city: Stuttgart), all pupils in schools of the 'secondary modern type' (catering for the less-academic half of the attainment range, *Hauptschulen*) are required to take leaving examinations in core subjects including mathematics, at an average age of just under sixteen. They can conveniently be compared with selected similar questions set to representative samples of pupils in England and Wales at an average age fifteen years and eight months by the Assessment of Performance Unit (APU) of the Department for Education.

These comparisons have the advantage for our purposes that the pupils are older than in the international surveys mentioned previously, and are near the end of their compulsory schooling; apprenticeship or traineeship is the next step for most of them in Germany. How well are they prepared for that step? A single example adequately illustrates the contrast between the countries. A simple add-and-subtract-sum (with both one and two decimal places) was set to English pupils by the APU:

$$2.6 - 4.12 + 6.3 - 0.44 = ?$$

It was answered correctly by a mere 24 per cent of *all* English pupils, that is, by pupils throughout the whole attainment range; for English pupils in the lower half of the attainment range, it has been estimated that a negligible 4 per cent would be able to answer correctly.[23] In German *Hauptschulen*, a similar but more difficult question was set in the leaving examinations for 1991, to be answered *without* calculators, as follows:-

$$5634.3 - 3194.02 + 4571.6 + 378.98 - 856.75 = ?$$

It was answered correctly by 76 per cent of pupils in those German schools. Only the top fifth of all English pupils, with 62 per cent correct, were able to approach the attainments of the German lowest two-fifths of all pupils. From a vocational point of view, arithmetical competence instilled at this level is helpful both to the craftsman who has to calculate his bills of quantities, as well as to the many other pupils in *Hauptschulen* who take up traineeships as accounts or sales assistants, for example.

Calculators and 'Modern Mathematics'

It is sometimes suggested that English pupils compensate – in some sense – for their deficiencies in arithmetic by excelling in other topics in mathematics, particularly questions on understanding bar-charts and pie-charts, or calculating simple averages – questions that are now often put under the pretentious heading of 'Data analysis, probability and statistics'. It is, however, more correct to say on the basis of these international tests that English pupils have not fallen as far behind in questions under that heading, probably because such questions in international tests were deliberately kept arithmetically very simple (for example, using only single-digit numbers in calculating averages). Thus, the 1990 IAEP comparisons for questions in this 'data analysis' category put England and Wales a little below Switzerland, indistinguishable from France, and a little ahead of Italy. Geometry is also sometimes mentioned as an area in which English pupils are 'strong'; but in geometrical questions in those 1990 comparisons, English pupils in fact came below France, Italy and Switzerland. Further, it must be remembered that the poorer cooperation of English schools in such comparisons is likely to have overstated the average attainments of English pupils.[24]

The introduction of pocket calculators is often advanced in Britain as a justification for the fall in pencil-and-paper and mental arithmetic. Calculators are now treated as compulsory in Britain under the National Curriculum, starting from primary school; but in other industrially highly successful countries – for example, Japan, Germany, Switzerland – concern that the child's mind needs first to become fully adept in basic arithmetical processes has led to an insistence on deferral in the use of calculators in school to the age of about fourteen. For the sake of clarity it should be added that everyone agrees that the use of calculators should be taught at school – the issue is the *correct age* for doing so.[25] The danger of too early a use of calculators was recently emphasised by Professor Geoffrey Howson (Professor Emeritus of Mathematical Curriculum Studies at the University of Southampton); as he put it: 'a child is likely to find the soroban or abacus more useful than a calculator for learning the fundamentals of number'.[26] Continental teachers and heads of training in places of employment, with whom this issue was discussed in the course of our research visits, condemned without exception the early introduction of calculators in schools because of its deleterious consequences for the development of pupils' mathematical capabilities.

The 'New Mathematics' (or 'Modern Mathematics') movement of the past generation must bear part of the responsibility for a continued low emphasis on arithmetic in English curricula, and for pupils' lower attainments. This movement attempted (a) to broaden the range of mathematical topics taught at early ages, by including topics until then considered suitable only at advanced level; and (b) to broaden the style of teaching, emphasising individualistic 'discovery' methods of learning and data-gathering – which absorb very much school-time – as against what was condemned as 'old-fashioned rote learning'. The beginnings of this movement are often traced to 1957 when *Sputnik* was launched, and Western countries felt a near-hysterical urge for a revolution in mathematics teaching in order 'to catch up with Russia'. But there were also important predecessors who started from notions of the natural psychological development of children's conceptual levels (Piaget), and from the logical foundations of mathematical knowledge (Bourbaki) – though it is questionable whether these notions have any great importance in deciding the optimum sequence of topics for classroom teaching. The movement gained strength following the 1959 OEEC conference on mathematics teaching held at Royaumont. A consequence of these changes was that learning time both at primary and secondary schools was directed away from proficiency in basic arithmetic towards newer approaches. These were seized upon strongly in Britain, partly because it coincided with the move towards comprehensive schools and mixed-ability teaching, and the latter required a search for new approaches to teaching.

Topics introduced as part of the New Mathematics movement included: set theory, alternative number bases, vectors, matrices, tessellations, symmetry, probability. Almost all this new material was originally intended for, and is of value to, academically inclined pupils proceeding to university degrees in mathematics or physics – rather than to the ordinary citizen in daily life and work. The new approach placed undue emphasis on highly abstract matters – the common logical structures permeating the foundations of a variety of mathematical topics – as against earlier approaches which concentrated on guiding pupils to mastering their everyday mathematical needs. The new topics could be taught to the majority of pupils only at a very elementary level; pupils were taught to recognise a new series of symbols, but the practical purpose of it all was largely beyond their horizon. It was as if they had been taught a new alphabet, but never reached the stage of making sensible words and sentences. (For example, matrix notation is marvellous in solving simultaneous linear equations in many variables; but merely learning the notation for the transpose of a matrix or the rules for multiplying two matrices, and stopping at that stage, is bound to be seen by most pupils as pointless.)

The new approach thus did not serve the immediate learning needs of average children, nor their needs when they became average citizens: did it help the specialised mathematician? An answer given some years ago by Dr J.M. Hammersley, FRS, of the University of Oxford, in an article in the *Bulletin of the Institution of Mathematics and its Applications* still seems to me correct; the title said it all: 'On the enfeeblement of mathematical skills by "Modern Mathematics" and by similar soft intellectual trash in schools and universities'. He judged the new emphasis to be 'didactically bad' and, in its extreme form, as 'having blunted the mathematical edge of a whole generation of children to an extent that we do not yet quite realise'.[27]

Some – but only some – of the new topics were subsequently withdrawn from school syllabuses, as if they were fashion items at the end of the season; but the unfortunate consequences for lowered arithmetical competences remain. They were reinforced by the 'discovery and investigative' methods of learning which continue to absorb much time in British schools. For example, English 11-year-old pupils are required to 'test the validity of statements such as . . . it is harder to get a six on a dice than a one'; and to 'observe from data they have collected that woodlice prefer dark, damp conditions because more of them are found under stones, damp rubbish, etc.' These examples are quoted verbatim from the National Curriculum in mathematics (revised version laid before Parliament in December 1991; Attainment Target 1: Using and Applying Mathematics, Level 4). Nothing corresponding to such activities was observed in Continental schools visited by the National Institute teams, nor was it found in their National Curricula or textbooks.

The legally obligatory Statement of Attainment to which these examples relate was expressed in the Statutory Order, very simply, in two words: 'Make generalisations'. If an English pupil is able to 'make generalisations' in this way, neither more nor less, he is to be assessed as having reached Level 4. He is to be down-labelled to Level 3 if he is able only to '*investigate* general statements by *trying out some examples*'; while if he is able to 'make a generalisation *and test it*', he is to be raised to Level 5. Differences between successive Levels, defined in this way for the National Curriculum, are supposed to correspond to a *two-year*(!) difference in an average child's attainments; a child is therefore to be categorised as having attainments corresponding to an average 9, 11 or 13-year-old on the basis of such subtle distinctions in generalising capabilities as judged by his or her teacher.[28]

A fifth of the total marks in mathematics was required by the National Curriculum (since its revision in December 1991) to be devoted to this investigative branch of the subject (misleadingly called 'Using and applying mathematics'), just as a fifth is to be devoted equally to each of the other four topics distinguished by the National Curriculum: Arithmetic (called Number in the National Curriculum), Algebra, Geometry (called Shape and Space) and Handling Data. It may seem surprising that the weightings devoted to these five topics should be equal; and even more surprising that the weightings are equal throughout the age range and throughout the attainment range. It contrasts with widely accepted teaching practices that a child should begin predominantly with arithmetic; and that even at secondary school for those who have difficulty in mathematics, the mastery of arithmetical topics is to be given priority. That remains the approach elsewhere, including the Continental schools we visited. Evidently the British National Curriculum was not given the degree of experienced advice that the task needed; no flexibility in degree of specialisation within the subject formed part of the vision of those who formulated the Curriculum.

Insofar as there may previously have been an over-concentration on routine practice of arithmetical sums devoid of any realistic context, it is understandable that educational reformers should call for more applied teaching. That is, in order that pupils should learn the circumstances when a particular technique is to be applied, it is helpful that mathematical questions in school are set in the context of counting apples, dividing cakes, angles of a ladder leaning against a wall, amps and volts, interest on capital, and pressures and volumes of a gas in a container. But this kind of contextual and realistic example needs to be clearly distinguished from the 'investigations' favoured by the National Curriculum approach, in which much time is to be spent by pupils collecting data which could just as well be given to them (counting the number of cars passing the school door, working out how the proportion of red cars varies during the day); or pursuing tedious open-ended abstract exercises with no practical significance (for example, which numbers cannot be expressed as the sum of three primes?).[29] Of course, teachers often find it convenient to provide brighter pupils with 'extension' exercises to keep them busy while weaker pupils are being helped in basics; but in English mathematics classes that need seems often to have reached unjustifiable levels. Such investigational exercises may then serve as convenient 'time-fillers' (or 'holding activities') to meet teachers' needs in that situation; it is not clear that they have served any other significant positive instructional purpose.[30]

We see, in short, that the teaching of mathematics in British schools has distinctive elements which have contributed to less emphasis on arithmetic – and thus, not surprisingly, to low attainments in that basic branch of mathematics. Many pupils consequently have had difficulties in other branches of mathematics and in those branches of science that rely on mathematical formulation (physics, in particular). It has put average and below-average school-leavers at a particular disadvantage in their subsequent technical and vocational training.[31]

Increasing the emphasis on arithmetic is obviously not the only change needed. On the basis of Continental teaching experience, matters outside the scope of curriculum specification also need attention. For example, more systematic remedial measures need to be put in place to reduce the proportion of stragglers at early ages; and there need to be changes in teaching styles to ensure that the whole class advances together (discussed further below), and so that the basic minimum for that class is mastered by virtually all pupils. Nevertheless, a greater emphasis on arithmetic – while not the whole remedy – would amount to a very significant simple first step towards closing the gap in mathematical attainments between Britain and the Continent; and it would contribute to a better foundation for the teaching at school of science, technology and practical subjects.

Practical subjects at school

A substantial proportion of Continental pupils, about a third of 14–16-year-olds, follow courses at secondary schools which provide them with a firm grounding in practical subjects – such as metalwork, technical drawing, engineering practice, textiles, or commercial practice – and which encourage them to proceed to traineeships leading to recognised vocational qualifications. Because of that grounding provided at secondary schools, it is also subsequently more advantageous for employers to take them on as trainees.

Differences in the organisational framework of Continental schools need to be taken into account at this stage. Secondary schools in many parts of the Continent (including Germany, the Netherlands and Switzerland – the countries visited most recently by the National Institute's teams) are separated, not into the two streams previously familiar in Britain (Grammar schools and Secondary Moderns), but into three or four streams varying from academic to vocationally oriented. The age of transfer to secondary schools varies from ten to twelve, and is now mostly about twelve. The choice of stream now usually lies ultimately with parents, acting on the advice of the primary school; but the parent is asked to bear in mind that opting for too academic a stream may involve class repetition for their child and consequent disappointment. A more or less common curriculum is characteristic of the initial year in the various streams to facilitate reassessment and change of streams; from about the age of fourteen there is increasing specialisation, with practical subjects featuring to a greater extent in vocationally oriented schools. In schools of the latter kind visited by National Institute teams, pupils from that age concentrate on *applied* aspects of their chosen practical subject: they learn the properties of the relevant raw materials and work on them, they learn to use correctly a range of basic tools, and they produce simple finished artefacts of high quality to given designs which they are proud to take home. The achievement of high quality in a specialised range of materials (for example, wood, metal or textiles) is more valued at that age than a great variety of materials worked on crudely and studied at a superficial level. Educationists and employers on the Continent value not only the basic specific occupational skills acquired by pupils in this way, but – perhaps even more – the acquisition of general 'good work habits' (called *Arbeitscharakter* by the Swiss) typified in terms of clean working, precision, perseverance, reliability and responsibility. As Continental teachers emphasised to us, it is also of great importance that many pupils, who otherwise would have difficulty in their academic subjects, improve in their academic subjects as a result of understanding acquired 'through their fingers' in practical subjects.[32]

Individualised projects rather than craft skills

British secondary schools in the past generation have gradually moved this part of their curriculum towards a more intellectualised approach. There is now an emphasis on general 'problem-solving skills', and on design and evaluation; pupils are set projects in highly generalised contexts (for example, how to give expression to a celebration), or involve over-complex contexts (for example, redesign an airport – a task set to 14-year-olds!).[33]

The new approach was given its fullest expression in the National Curriculum for Technology issued in March 1990. It soon led to great difficulties. The so-called 'problem-solving' approach required each pupil to pursue an *individual* response to a theme or problem specified only in the very broadest terms. Inevitably there were difficulties in teaching the class as a whole and in supervising it. In addition, the NC required a great range of *materials* to be used by each pupil, and a great range of *products* in a great range of *contexts*.[34] This led to inadequate specialisation, inadequate progression, and poor quality of finished work; breadth was to be pursued at the expense of specialised depth and high standards.

A further feature of this approach was that the element of actual *making* in practical subjects in British schools was marginalised – in practice, often trivialised into so-called '*Blue Peter*' technology and 'cardboard engineering'. Broadly speaking, only an eighth of the total marks for the obligatory components of Design and Technology in the National Curriculum (1990) was awarded for actual *making*. It thus became hardly possible for average 16-year-old pupils in British schools to develop their practical skills to standards current on the Continent; those standards had previously been attained in Britain in many secondary schools where specialised practical subjects were taken at GCSE examinations. School-leavers in the less-academic half of the attainment range were particularly disadvantaged and demotivated.

A revision of this part of the National Curriculum was ordered by the Secretary of State in the summer of 1992. Proposals resulting from a series of consultations led to a series of interim simplifications; at the time of this writing a fuller revision is expected at the end of 1994, and it remains unclear whether the kind of specialised practical course previously taken at GCSE – whether on the commercial or technical sides – will be permitted in English schools for 14–16-year-olds. Whatever the eventual outcome, at this stage we have to recognise that this part of British schooling – combined with poor mathematical attainments at school – has contributed to the difficulties that British school-leavers have faced in attaining the wider technical competence characteristic of Continental workforces.

Organisation of schooling

The higher and more even attainments of Continental pupils – when compared with English pupils on international tests – are partly related to difference in curriculum objectives, as explained above. In addition, there are important differences between English and Continental schools in classroom organisation, in teachers' attitudes to pupils' variability of attainments, in teaching styles (as well as in subject specialisation, as just mentioned) – all of which combine to bear on pupils' attainments. This section outlines the most significant of such organisational differences as observed by the Institute's teams on their visits to Continental schools in the early 1990s (the teams consisted of highly experienced teachers and school inspectors, as well as Institute researchers). The main objective of those visits – in line with themes developed in previous chapters of this book – was to focus on aspects of schooling that help raise the achievements particularly of pupils in the lower sections of the academic attainment range. It is hoped that the brief description given here of these aspects – some perhaps fairly obvious, others hardly written about elsewhere – will provide a stimulus to a reconsideration of some established English practices.[35]

Standards expected

The attitude of teachers on the Continent towards the required achievement of the range of pupils in their class differs from those in Britain: their prime aim is to ensure that virtually all pupils reach a basic standard as set out in their curriculum for each year-group (as will be explained further in a moment, the National Curriculum in England is less clear since it deals with a group of years at a time). Continental teachers thus know what they can expect their pupils to have learnt in the previous class, and can build on it with greater confidence. The teaching of new topics is therefore more efficient. Additional instructional time and resources are used to bring slower pupils to the class's standard of achievement: if necessary, some pupils are given 'remedial' lessons to reach those standards – whether in normal school hours or outside these hours; on occasions pupils repeat a year, but only rarely (say, one pupil a year in each class on average).[36]

In contrast, teachers in England place greater emphasis on catering for, and stimulating, individual pupils' differences; this applies from an early age. Virtually all pupils born in a given twelve-month period spend a calendar year in each class, and then move on to the next class *irrespective of their attainments*. The ten 'Levels of Attainment' specified in the National Curriculum reflect the English concern to encourage individuality in pupils from an early age. Under National Curriculum arrangements, as explained in the previous section, each level is supposed to correspond to two years of learning by the average child; and the middle 80 per cent of children at age eleven, for example, are expected to vary in their attainments between National Curriculum Levels 2–3 and 5–6, corresponding to the attainments of average achievers between ages eight and fourteen. (The remaining 20 per cent of children are expected to have attainments that lie outside even that wide range.)

Pupils of such widely varying attainments are usually all taught in the same classroom in England (at the primary level, for all subjects; at the secondary level, exceptions are now usually made for mathematics and foreign languages – for which classes are 'set' by attainment). The teacher has no effective response to make to pupils whose pace is simply too slow in relation to their capabilities, and are content – as educationalists say – to proceed 'at their own pace'. Incentives for pupils, parents and teachers to strive for standards that a teacher considers appropriate for that class as a whole, are consequently weaker than on the Continent. Teaching the class as a *single whole* becomes more difficult, sometimes even impossible, in these circumstances for most subjects; and it becomes more difficult the older the pupils are, since the diversity of attainments increases cumulatively with age. Individualised teaching, or teaching to separate groups within a classroom, is the response that teachers in England consequently find it necessary to adopt.

Continental National Curricula specify for *each year* the topics to be taught and the appropriate level of difficulty; the nearest we reach towards this in the English National Curriculum is in terms of legislated 'Programmes of Study' covering each 'Key Stage' of schooling. There are important differences. First, a Key Stage covers 2–4 years of schooling; the longest stage of four years until recently was in junior schools and covered 8–11-year-olds, that is, Years 3–6. The revised mathematics National Curriculum issued in November 1994 treats the whole *five* years of secondary schooling together (that is, the previous Key Stages 3 and 4 are to be merged), so that no teaching objectives are specified for anything other than for the whole eleven to sixteen age-group. Each year of schooling is usually taught in England by a different teacher, who therefore cannot tell from the National Curriculum documentation what pupils should be expected to have learnt in the previous year, nor is it laid down – as a minimum core requirement or otherwise – what should be taught in the coming year. This aspect of English legislation on the curriculum clearly does not provide as effectively as on the Continent for coherence of teaching between successive years of schooling.

A second difference is that Continental curricula specify more precisely what is to be taught and learnt; in England, possibly because of the fear of encouraging unduly narrow 'teaching to the test', the National Curriculum is formulated in terms of very broad targets such as (to quote again the extreme example of a 'Statement of Attainment' given above for mathematics in primary schools): 'Make generalisations'. These provide the teacher with inadequate operational precision.

The greater emphasis on the Continent on evenness of pupils' *attainments* within each class carries the consequence that pupils' *ages* vary more than here. Age-spans within a class of a full two years were not unusual in the Swiss and German secondary schools we visited, in contrast to a fairly strict one-year span found in England. On the Continent the better chance of slow-developing pupils reaching satisfactory school-leaving standards if put in a younger class is valued more highly than their being put in a class closer to their age – but with which it is difficult to keep pace. For the sake of clarity perhaps it needs to be said that the greater evenness of pupils' attainments on the Continent is not based on aiming at some low minimum standard; rather, evenness of a class's attainments is recognised as an essential part of the mechanism for attaining high average standards for the class as a whole.

Teaching style

Teachers on the Continent use a distinct teaching style which might be called 'interactive whole-class teaching'. This is not a form of lecturing, nor is it individualised learning in the sense that every child is left 'to work at their own pace' and is engaged on something different. For the central part of each lesson the Continental teacher employs question-and-answer methods which aim to maintain the attention of the whole class and to develop their understanding of the learning objectives of that lesson.[37]

The time-shape of a Continental lesson can be schematised as follows: revision of yesterday's lesson or of homework; new material outlined to the whole class by the teacher with the help of structured problems, during which individual pupils help to take the lesson forward in successive small steps on the blackboard (or overhead projector) on a question-and-answer approach, involving other pupils at successive steps or when difficulties arise; pupils practise exercises in their notebooks, but for a significantly smaller fraction of the total lesson time (well under half) than in England; finally, the main points of the lesson are gone over to 'fix' them in pupils' minds. The overriding aim is that *the whole class should advance together*, and this seems to be achieved by these methods to a remarkable extent. It seems that this Continental teaching style is of long standing.[38]

Teachers in England, especially in primary schools, teach very differently. They are encouraged through their training to attempt to 'meet the individual needs of pupils' through classroom grouping arrangements of great complexity; for example, groups of pupils sit at separate tables and may be working at the same time and in the same classroom in four or more different areas of the curriculum (for example, history, mathematics, pottery, English).[39] Teachers in England have been trained to attach great value to spontaneity and to open-ended investigative activity-based methods of learning. The latter partly fulfil the essential role of 'holding activities' (or time-fillers), keeping the rest of the class occupied while the teacher attempts to deal with individual pupils' problems. Within each lesson there is often a change of 'activity periods', each lasting about a quarter of an hour; much time is absorbed by associated reorganisational tasks, with children moving from one subject to another and from a table in one corner of the room to sitting on a carpet in another corner. When an English teacher addresses the class as a whole, it is more often to explain new groupings of pupils and the next range of tasks which pupils are to carry out, rather than to engage in direct instruction. Many teachers find the complexity unmanageable; but, with time, they become resigned to the system. In general, average 'contact-time' between each pupil and the teacher is much below that in the Continental approach to whole-class teaching, and pupils' learning time is far from effectively deployed.[40] Those pupils who are slow learners need more attention but often cannot receive it from the teacher busy dealing with so many individual needs; such pupils become discouraged and tend to fall increasingly behind from year to year. The system thus encourages the growth of pools of under-educated, frustrated and disaffected children.

English teaching methods, as they have recently evolved, may be understood as being a rational short-term response by the majority of teachers to the great diversity of pupils' attainments which they have inherited from previous classes attended by those pupils; but their own teaching methods, in turn, on the whole serve to reinforce and extend that diversity.[41]

Mental and oral work

The process of Continental teaching with its substantially greater component of pupils' contribution to the progress of the lesson, from their desk and even more so at the blackboard, promotes more coherent and correct speaking. This is especially important for children from homes where a local dialect or a minority language is spoken, and where there are social and cultural impediments at home; it thus promotes more even attainments within the class. The acquisition of better speaking skills helps such children overcome their difficulties, and it obviously also helps them in an important way when they come to seek employment.

In mathematics, as part of the interactive whole-class teaching approach, oral and mental work is given much greater prominence on the Continent (probably over half the lesson time). Mental arithmetic is often not taught systematically in England; where it is taught, it is often tacked on *after* written arithmetic has been mastered. On the Continent, the process seems to be reversed: mental arithmetic comes first; only afterwards are more difficult sums treated on a pencil-and-paper approach.[42]

Textbooks

Textbooks are relied upon to a fundamentally greater extent in Continental than in English schools. In order to understand this difference properly, it is worth spelling out the extreme ways in which textbooks combine with syllabus requirements to help the teaching process. At one extreme the class may use no published textbook at all and rely on duplicated sheets prepared by the teacher, or by the teacher's associates and predecessors at the school; or the teacher may even rely solely on oral instruction. At the other extreme there is the 'open your textbook at page 67' approach; each pupil has a textbook, homework is set from that book, and parents consequently know and can help with what is being taught. In between are schools that use textbooks some of the time. Often in English schools not enough copies of the same textbooks are available for each pupil: different books are thus used simultaneously in the class, and one book may be shared between two pupils 'to encourage group working'; pupils are not usually permitted to take textbooks home, especially during the primary phase. The lack of textbooks in English schools is sometimes attributed to the need for economy. But ideological elements also enter: textbooks are said to cramp the individuality of the teaching process, and teachers are thus encouraged to design their own worksheets; there is also a view that it is better for parents not to know too precisely what is taught, since parents' help may lead to inequitable progress among pupils, or may use different methods which could confuse the child.

In Continental countries, textbooks are sometimes authorised or recommended by the local education authority and, in effect, serve as a more detailed – but not obligatory – supplement to their legislated curricula. There are often also extensive teachers' manuals, perhaps three times the size of pupils' books. The teacher is not obliged to use the approved textbook, nor indeed any textbook, so long as the main material in the recommended textbooks is covered. The time and importance attached to the various topics and the method or style of teaching are, in principle, left to the Continental teacher.

The extent of textbook usage varies according to subject; for example, pupils' textbooks are hardly used in craftwork – though a teacher's manual of suitable projects is usually provided. On the other hand, in mathematics and science we found that pupils on the Continent invariably were supplied with their own textbooks, and were expected to take them home for homework; sometimes additional duplicated sheets (for 'reinforcement' exercises) were supplied by the teacher. Our teams were left in little doubt that the more intensive way that textbooks support learning at schools on the Continent (that is, combined with their 'interactive teaching style') contributed substantially to the avoidance of the degree of under-achievement seen so frequently in English schools.

Length of lesson

Lessons on the Continent typically take 45 minutes, rather than the 35-minute 'single lesson', or 'double lesson' time of 1 hour 10 minutes, now frequently adopted by schools in England. The former is too short; and latter is too long for most pupils in subjects such as mathematics which require extended mental concentration.

Fixed classrooms

Pupils in most secondary schools in the Continental countries we visited have their 'own' desks in a fixed classroom in which they receive the majority of their lessons. In most secondary schools now in Britain, pupils move from one classroom to another according to the subject being taught (this is also so in those comprehensive schools on the Continent that we visited; but there are very few of these, as discussed further below). Much time is taken up by this peripatetic approach; some pupils 'get lost' from one lesson to the next (leading to truancy and its consequences). The attendance register thus needs to be taken more frequently, sometimes whenever a class begins; and varying class sizes often require movement of desks and chairs from one room to another to provide adequate accommodation. Learning time under these conditions is used inefficiently. In some English primary schools, the only fixed point for a pupil is a small drawer in a corner for their belongings, and otherwise they move around the classroom.

The lack of a pupil's fixed place is considered by Continental teachers to be particularly disadvantageous for pupils who come from difficult home backgrounds. Such pupils value the psychological consequences of the fixity of their desks, the assurance provided by having familiar neighbours around them, and the greater 'sense of belonging' to their own classroom. The welfare and educational progress of weaker pupils deserves emphasis not only because of their own interests – which are of course very important – but also because their neglect has consequences for the orderliness and learning efficiency of the class as a whole. To put it simply, if some pupils in the class fall behind, other pupils also suffer because the teacher's attention has to be directed to help those who are lagging.

The role of the form teacher

Differences in the role of the form teacher between the Continent and Britain are particularly marked at the secondary level. A Continental secondary school teacher tends to teach more subjects than in this country; most Continental classes – that is, apart from those in grammar schools – have only one or two teachers for most subjects (for example, one teacher will be responsible for most 'arts' subjects, and another for mathematics and science subjects). Specialist teachers and specialist classrooms are usually involved only for gymnastics, music or craftwork (sciences are sometimes taught in the laboratory, but not always). In consequence of the form teacher teaching so many more subjects, there is closer contact and deeper understanding by the Continental form teacher of his or her individual pupils than in England: the form teacher becomes more familiar with a

pupil's home and personal circumstances, will be more sensitive to problems that may have arisen, will know when to advise (and when it is better not to advise), knows personally the relative strengths of the pupil in
different subjects, and eventually will be able to provide better guidance
on career choice. This stronger pastoral role contributes to greater cohe-
sion of the class; problems leading to a pupil's disaffection can be caught
at an early stage, and not allowed to grow to the point where they inter-
fere with that cooperative whole-class learning atmosphere evident on entering a Continental classroom.

At the primary level in England the form teacher teaches almost all subjects, as on the Continent. Because of the greater demands of the National
Curriculum there are now moves to encourage teachers to become subject
specialists in England even at the primary level. The broader education of
primary school teachers on the Continent – particularly because of the wide
curriculum of some ten subjects required at what corresponds to their A–
levels (*Baccalauréat, Abitur*) – provides sufficient mastery for there to be
no need for subject specialists on the Continent. It seems that the degree
of sixth-form specialisation of those planning to be teachers warrants fuller
comparisons with the Continent.

School size

Secondary schools on the Continent tend to be significantly smaller, aver-
aging under 500 pupils compared with over 1,000 in Britain. The more
personal atmosphere in a smaller school inhibits disaffection and 'fester-
ing sores' which otherwise gradually spread and pull down a school's ethos
and its pupils' attainments. Inevitably, it is the weaker pupils' who are particularly disadvantaged by such problems.

Continental schools are of a size such that the head teacher knows all
the pupils; because of their smaller size, there is less need for a hierarchy
of levels of control of the kind found in large English schools, with ensuing diffusion of responsibility and the need for a multiplicity of co-
ordinators of various sorts (pastoral, supervisory, careers, individual
subjects). Problems are consequently dealt with more rapidly and more
effectively.[43]

Pathways and specialisation of schools

The smaller size of secondary schools on the Continent is accompanied by
less choice of optional subjects within a school; correspondingly, there is a
greater variety of curricula among school types. That is to say (as indicated
in the section above, where we discussed the teaching of practical subjects),

Continental secondary schools tend to be more specialised according to pupils' interests and capabilities. With rising prosperity, and employers' growing demands for more advanced schooling attainments to cope with modern production methods, the average age at which pupils leave full-time schooling has tended to rise in all countries; and this has been accompanied by a rise in the age at which decisions are taken for entry to different types of secondary school. The detailed pattern of organisation varies considerably, but the following can probably be taken as the broad pattern.

Continental *primary* schools tend to be 'comprehensive' in their intake, as in Britain (that is, they cater for the full range of pupils' attainments); and there is no streaming by ability. They may take pupils up to the age of twelve, which is a year older than usual in England; in areas where the age of ten is the top class in primary school, the first two years of secondary school tend to be treated as an 'orientation' phase, during which decisions as to final type of secondary school can more easily be reconsidered. From the age of about fourteen, Continental schooling systems provide more distinct curricula, embodying varying vocational or technical pathways in addition to the academic pathway; the Dutch system is particularly specialised and diverse, and their vocational and technical secondary schools (catering for ages twelve to sixteen) have admirable specialised 'workshops' and well developed teaching materials for practical subjects.

The kind of large comprehensive secondary school typical of Britain is found much less frequently in the Continental countries we visited (catering for under a tenth of pupils in Switzerland and Germany); where it exists, it tends to be closer to the multilateral form of organisation typical of the earlier years of comprehensivisation in England (with streams covering most subjects, according to ability level), rather than to the mixed-ability type now typical of English secondary schools. While debates on comprehensivisation continue on the Continent, more emphasis seems to be given to strengthening bridges between the different types of secondary school (and between the different streams within comprehensive schools) so as to improve provision for pupils who are late developers or wish to change their career paths. Crossing the bridge to a different type of secondary school may involve repeating a year of schooling in order to cover specialised aspects of the curriculum not previously covered.

In the curricula for Continental vocationally oriented secondary schools, whether pre- or post-16, general schooling subjects (native language, mathematics) retain their independence, rather than being integrated or implicit parts of vocational subjects, as is the tendency in English post-16 education. Standards attained in general subjects form essential elements of final awards, together with pupils' attainments on practical and vocational subjects. Vocational guidance at such schools is given at an earlier age (say, from thirteen) and is more occupationally specific than in England; it provides pupils with greater motivation at school for success in a broad range of subjects so as to gain access to more demanding work.[44]

Continental secondary schools do not attempt to provide a single final school-leaving qualification in separate subjects for all pupils, as does the GCSE with its wide-ranging levels of attainment A–G (the lower of which provide doubtful incentives for weaker pupils to work more effectively). Rather, each school type has a distinct school-leaving certificate covering jointly a group of specified core subjects with syllabuses appropriate for each level. The school-leaving certificate is a document of prime importance for employment; and it is intended to provide a clear foundation for pupils who wish to attend further vocational courses and advance to a more highly skilled career.

Many of the organisational features that have been selected here as distinctive of Continental schooling are interdependent and mutually reinforcing. They combine in complex ways to reduce the variability of pupils' attainments, to make the task of school teacher more manageable, and to raise the general standard of pupils' attainments. It is thus not easy to arrange them in order of importance, nor in order of priority for policy purposes. They need, rather, all to be viewed as issues which, step by step, need to be reconsidered in the British context as possible routes by which the efficiency of the schooling process can be improved.

5   From principles to practice

Problems of transition

Ultimate objectives may be clear enough, and agreed on all sides: but attempts to change long-established features of a socio-economic system have to overcome a host of stumbling blocks that often are linked and mutually supporting. Our main concern in this chapter is thus not the rehearsal of an all-embracing list of long-term policy priorities, but rather to indicate the nature of the detailed practical transitional issues, the resolution of which is likely to require many further years of debate. While previous chapters have related to problems common to both Britain and many other industrially developed countries – problems of how to benefit more rapidly from advancing automation, of adjusting to increasing competition from developing low-wage economies, and of high unemployment amongst the young and unskilled – this chapter deals with issues in their detailed institutional context in Britain, though parallels are often to be recognised in other countries.

Much has been done by the British government in the past decade in attempts to improve training and schooling that might previously have been considered beyond the bounds of domestic political acceptability. The central elements were the introduction of massive subsidies to vocational training through the Youth Training Scheme and its successors, financial support to schools to improve technical and vocational teaching (through TVEI financed, remarkably enough, via the Department of Employment), and measures to raise school-leaving attainments through the specification of a National Curriculum for schools together with nationwide testing of pupils' attainments. Despite a succession of revisions, these important reforms are still some way from meeting their objectives, perhaps largely because they did not allow for the heavy inertia of the existing system and for the need to plan detailed transitional measures. It might also be said that many features of these recent British reforms were unduly 'original' and contained flaws which might have been avoided had more attention been paid to the experience of Continental neighbours (in the nature of a reluctance to adopt wheels if they had been invented elsewhere). Notwithstanding extensive moves in this period towards greater European economic, social and political integration, convergence to common European basic schooling and training standards remains hardly perceptible.

Long-evident issues

The underlying policy issues of previous chapters may perhaps be summarised in three principal propositions. First, in developed economies there is a general need for intervention by government (or by other social institutions) to support vocational training. Leaving it solely to market forces is unlikely to be adequate because, for example, (a) existing subsidies to university courses – often academic – tempt young persons away from vocational traineeships; (b) inadequate capital resources and inadequate foresight restrain the young from investing in their future training; (c) long-established high wages expected by the young in England make it uneconomic for employers to provide training with the technological depth needed by modern industry and at the same time offer an acceptable wage.

Second, we have seen that governmental subsidies for training need to be focused, not on job skills specific to an individual employer, but on systematic courses for careers combining both a broad base of transferable knowledge and skills (for example, in engineering, commerce) and occupationally specific knowledge and skills (for example, in toolmaking or mechanical maintenance; travel agency or personnel office).

Third, learning objectives during the period of full-time schooling in Britain need to be moved, not towards preparing an increased number of young people to enter academic university courses, but towards providing the great majority of school-leavers with attainments suited for subsequent skilled vocational training, in the way long familiar on the Continent.

Policies to put such changes into effect have become more urgent with the growth of automation; in considering what still needs doing today, it is as well to remind ourselves again that the underlying trends have been evident for over a century to those who had carefully observed steps taken by Continental countries to catch up with Britain's earlier extraordinary achievements in leading the industrial revolution.

A greater orientation of Continental schooling towards the requirements of working life was increasingly noted by British observers as the nineteenth century progressed, and led to a series of important Parliamentary Commissions of Inquiry. These repeatedly drew attention in particular to Germany's rapid industrial development, and to the need for Britain to emulate Continental approaches to education. 'Our evidence appears to show,' said the Taunton Commission as long ago as 1868, 'that our industrial classes have not even that basis of sound general education on which alone technical instruction can rest.' 'Even if such schools [for technical instruction] were generally established among us, there is reason to fear that they would fail to produce any valuable results for want . . . of sound elementary knowledge of the learners.' The urgent need, as they saw it, was for schools which gave teachers 'considerable freedom in the use of methods, but [defined] the chief aim and purpose clearly and precisely, and that aim should be thoroughly to satisfy the demands of the parents for good elementary teaching, and then, and only then, to add anything more.'[1]

These themes were reinforced by subsequent Parliamentary inquiries (the Devonshire Commission, 1872; the Samuelson Commission, 1882–4; the Bryce Commission, 1895). In 1890 the great Cambridge economist Alfred Marshall published his *Principles of Economics*, in the early editions of which he drew attention to the virtues of Continental systems of education: 'On the whole we may say that at present England is very much behind hand as regards the provision for the commercial as well as the technical education of the proprietors and principal managers of industrial works'; the German system in particular had produced men 'who are better fitted to do the work required of the middle ranks of industry than any that the world has ever seen'.[2] A subsequent and more detailed study contrasting industry and trade in Britain with the United States, France and Germany was published by Marshall in 1919; in discussing the foundations of industrial progress, he still felt it right to say – notwithstanding the terrible war against Germany that had only just ended – that 'all the world has much to learn from German methods of education'; and that 'the same may perhaps be said of Scandinavia and Switzerland'.[3]

Developments at the end of the nineteenth century in Britain included funding for higher-grade elementary schools (above the age of twelve), for science schools and junior technical schools, and for continuing part-time education; the possibility of legally obligatory day release from work for two years after compulsory full-time schooling – subject to agreement by the local education authority – was introduced under the 1918 Fisher Education Act, but was put into practice only on a very limited scale.[4] Lengthening of compulsory full-time schooling gradually followed, from the age of twelve at the beginning of this century to sixteen today; technical secondary schools (for 12–16-year-olds) advanced further in the 1920s (as mentioned in chapter 4), but virtually disappeared with the move towards comprehensive schooling in the 1960s.

Britain has now inherited a general full-time schooling system in which there is considerably less provision than on the Continent for those who wish to enter the world of work shortly after completing compulsory full-time schooling, and for whom some kind of traineeship or apprenticeship provides an appropriate ladder for advancing their understanding and skills. Many of the differences from the Continent noted as warranting change a century ago still seem relevant today. There is obviously much persistence and inertia in the institutional arrangements that transmit educational values from one generation to the next; and much patient chopping away at one detailed resistant difficulty after another is needed.[5]

Vocational training

In attempting in the past decade to promote the take-up of systematic and reliably certificated vocational training, the British government rightly focused on the need to improve the organisational structure of vocational qualifications and on the incentives to acquire them. Nevertheless, severe unresolved problems continue to attach to the content of vocational courses and the testing and certification of skills in Britain.

Certification

While the acquisition of skills – irrespective of their certification – carries its own rewards, better certification procedures help both employers and employees: employers are prepared to pay premia for skills, and higher premia if they are reliably certificated; and school-leavers benefit by being able to take those higher premia into account in deciding which occupation it is worth training for. In other words, the establishment of reliable 'hallmarks' within a widely recognised framework improves their marketability. If qualifications are awarded with inadequate safeguards for objectivity and reliability, it is hardly surprising to hear complaints of 'lack of esteem' for vocational qualifications.

Externally marked written and practical tests, based on apprenticeship and part-time college attendance, have for long formed accepted preconditions on the Continent for the award of craft-level vocational qualifications, and continue to do so today; they were equally the objectives to which qualifications in Britain were moving (such as the combined certificate of the City and Guilds and the Engineering Industry Training Board). However, when the National Council for Vocational Qualifications was established in 1986, it decided to rely almost entirely on assessment by the trainee's workplace supervisor of a narrow range of skills: there was excessive concern with the immediate needs of the individual employer, rather than the long-term needs of the market for skills as a whole, and there was little concern with the wider understanding of general principles that help an apprentice to master his trade and be able to respond to changing circumstances and changing technologies. External testing of the individual candidate to ensure reliability and marketability of the qualification, breadth of vocational field to promote flexibility, written components of examinations to encourage mastery of general principles – all are now less adequate in Britain following NCVQ reforms than they used to be, and are far from accepted Continental procedures. The current approach in Britain is closer to the notion of a narrowly defined skill certificate for a specific *job*: it is to be distinguished from the transferable career training – comprising a broad base plus specialisation – characteristic of the Continental system of vocational training and qualification.

More recent moves to develop broader General National Vocational Qualifications in relation to approximately a dozen 'occupational families' indicate a recognition of the need for breadth; these newer qualifications are based on full-time college-based courses, rather than on workplace-based training. This approach has long been recognised as suitable for preparation for office and similar occupations. But it is not necessarily a good way to inculcate the practical basics of manufacturing or construction competences, particularly for that great proportion of British school-leavers who do not thrive in a school setting. The few GNVQs that have so far (as at end-1994) been developed on a trial basis have been widely criticised for lack of clarity in content and lack of objectivity in final testing. A fundamental rethinking of the structural foundations for the award of vocational qualifications in Britain is still necessary if they are to carry the objectivity, marketability and esteem that they have on the Continent (the introduction of GNVQs in secondary schools is considered further below).[6]

Incentives

Financial subsidies for the training of young persons have been increased by the government in the past decade (under a variety of Youth Training Schemes) to close to a third of the adult wage. While trainee wages in Britain are considerably higher than on the Continent (nearly two-thirds rather than one-third of an adult's wage), the net cost of a trainee to a British employer after allowing for the subsidy is now often much the same as on the Continent. Nevertheless, these increases in financial incentives have not been adequate to yield as yet an increase in the numbers trained to recognised craft levels (NVQ Level 3). Some of that failing may be attributable to the deficiencies in the new structure of qualifications just mentioned; and some may be attributable to long time-lags in the labour market in adjusting to new incentives, and to a lack of confidence in their permanence.

Whatever the reason, alternative incentives need to be considered. One possibility would be to reimpose a 'self-financing' training levy on employers, repayable to those who provided training of appropriate standard; the rate of levy would be variable to ensure an adequate supply of training places and that they were taken up. A levy of this kind was introduced in Britain some twenty years ago, but was abandoned after a few years because of lack of clarity on skill levels to be attained and bureaucratic complexity. It needs to be reconsidered in the light of a reformed structure of vocational qualifications. The French training levy of 1–2 per cent of a firm's total wage bill, payable in cash or in kind, provides a valuable current example. German experience is also relevant in the way advance estimates are provided annually by employers of the total number of training places they propose to offer in order to match the expected number of school-leavers; a training levy on employers was under legislative consideration in Germany when a shortage of training places was in prospect about a decade ago, but has so far not had to be imposed.

The time has probably also come to consider again whether part-time vocational education and training should be made compulsory for a year or two for those leaving school in Britain at the end of full-time compulsory education, as in some Continental countries.[7] Two years is the current legal requirement for part-time vocational education in the Netherlands (two days a week at sixteen, one day a week at seventeen). The legal requirement in Germany used to be three years' part-time vocational education for one day a week until the age of eighteen; there is now usually an option of substituting one year's full-time vocational education, but the great majority of youngsters continue to follow the long-established three-year part-time route.

In Britain, with so much truancy among low-attaining pupils in the final years of compulsory schooling, it may well be inappropriate to extend the obligation of attendance at vocational courses even on a part-time basis; it is precisely that group of low-attaining school-leavers who would tend to resist legal obligations to attend further-education courses. The following measures might, however, be considered: (a) employers could be prohibited from employing anyone under seventeen unless the employment is of an approved trainee nature, combined with day release to attend a vocationally relevant course at a College of Further Education (that is to say, any legislative obligation is better placed on employers, rather than on employees); (b) after pupils have reached the age of fifteen they should, with the agreement of their secondary school head teacher, be entitled to move to such traineeship arrangements.

Continental training practice requires trainees to be under the supervision of a qualified master-craftsman acting as workplace trainer (in Germany, for example, a *Meister* is someone who has completed apprenticeship examinations, has had three years' subsequent practical experience, and has then taken additional part-time *Meister*-level courses for two years on technical, supervisory and didactic matters, and has passed final examinations). Such requirements cannot be put into effect in Britain for the foreseeable future for lack of suitably qualified persons; little thought has as yet been given to these aspects in policy discussion in Britain. A long-term scheme will need to be developed for the progressive raising of the minimum qualifications of a workplace trainer, perhaps as an extension of the current Department of Employment scheme for certifying approved employers as Investors in People.

Information

The improvement of information on skills – namely, on those who have gained certificated skills, on the appropriate courses for the acquisition of skills, and on the rewards for skills – provides further means which properly lie within the province of social action for encouraging higher levels of training in Britain. In many parts of the Continent those skilled occupations which serve the general public, such as electrician, plumber or mechanic, are required to be under the supervision of a certificated master- craftsman; such a requirement improves service to the public, and raises the esteem and financial rewards attached to the acquisition of certificated skills. To avoid monopolistic practices, any such requirement introduced in Britain today should be designed *not* to exclude non-accredited persons from working in those occupations – it would be sufficient if the market mechanism led such non-accredited practitioners to being paid less (misrepresentation would of course be illegal). The public would benefit by being provided with relevant information on the capabilities of such a craftsman, in the same way in which it benefits from other 'hallmarking' schemes.

So that youngsters do not begin vocational courses for which they are not suited, better information on entry requirements for vocational courses is also desirable together with checks that these entry requirements are adequately enforced.[8] All too often entry requirements are not tightly specified with the result that some entrants find that their basic school attainments prove inadequate to the demands of their courses, while others find the course too easy in relation to what they already know. Greater efficiency is to be gained by (a) requiring vocational colleges to specify their minimum entry requirements for each course more strictly (in terms of GCSE subjects and grades, or equivalents), so that trainees are less likely to choose courses that are unsuitable for them; (b) requiring colleges to publish an annual analysis of drop-outs and failures in relation to their students' entry qualifications; and (c) requiring colleges to raise entry requirements if failures are above some minimum.

Finally, there is a need for better information on earnings differentials according to certificated vocational qualification levels, to provide clearer incentives for those considering entry to courses leading to vocational qualifications. The Department of Employment publishes average earnings by industry, occupation, and so on; but it does not publish earnings classified according to vocational qualification. It should be possible to extend the *New Earnings Survey* to include earnings of those with specific examined vocational qualifications in adequate detail (for example, City and Guilds Part II mechanics) for comparison with unqualified workers of the same age.

Schooling

Vocational standards of the workforce in Britain, and the efficiency with which those standards are attained, cannot be expected to approach those of the Continent until school-leaving attainments in Britain – of average and below-average pupils – are raised very substantially so as to provide a better foundation for subsequent training. In considering policy measures to improve the effectiveness of the large resources invested by taxpayers in compulsory schooling, and of the valuable time invested by young people in their schooling, it is necessary to bear in mind a fundamental difference in the emphasis on individualised teaching that has arisen between British and Continental school practices. Especially in larger classes, there is typically a conflict as to how teachers should divide their limited time between teaching the class as a whole, and the more time-costly process of trying to provide individualised 'learning programmes' for each pupil. In

Britain emphasis has increasingly been placed in the past generation on a child-centred, individualistic approach to schooling in which the teaching of the whole class – especially in primary schools — occupies a small part of the time; on the Continent greater emphasis continues to be placed on teaching the class as a whole, though at the same time there have been moves to provide greater support for pupils with difficulties and special talents. As we have seen in chapter 4, in the final result the Continental approach has led to better schooling attainments on the whole, and especially for those in the lower part of the attainment range.

Depending partly on the pressures of local needs and circumstances, such as the growth in the proportion of children from single-parent families or from homes with immigrant language problems, the balance of teaching has shifted everywhere in recent decades towards a greater degree of individualised teaching within the classroom. In addition, teachers on the Continent as much as in Britain often have a continuing deep concern to overturn what they regard as symptoms or residues of authoritarian ideals of social organisation, and to promote democratic participative ideals in the process of classroom teaching. This too has led teachers to see their roles more as facilitators of individual pupils' learning than as leaders of the class as a whole. Just how and where to draw the line between the advancement of the individual pupil and the advancement of the class as a whole remains a continuing issue of experiment and debate.

As discussed at greater length in chapter 4, the difference between the British and the Continental approaches to teaching expresses itself in many ways – in the structure of the curriculum, in classroom organisation, in teaching styles, and in the availability and use of textbooks. The need for Britain to reap the benefits of agreed core learning objectives and co-ordinated syllabus timing (for example, in which year of schooling should the Norman invasion be taught, and for how many years is it necessary to repeat that topic?), led to detailed legislation on the curriculum at the end of the 1980s. But this did not bring British schooling practice very close to that on the Continent. Continental national curricula provide the teacher with guidance as to what is to be taught in each year of schooling, but the British National Curriculum was formulated in terms of Levels of Attainment and in terms of groups of years known as Key Stages. Each level is supposed to cover what an average child may be expected to learn in two years; and in each class – and this needs to be recognised as the crucial point – the teacher is expected to provide teaching for three or four such levels. In this way the National Curriculum legislation has, if anything, consolidated existing British tendencies to provide within each class for a much greater variability of attainment than on the Continent; the task of the average teacher in Britain thus continues to be more difficult than those of Continental counterparts.

The specification of curriculum content for a group of years together (in broad Key Stages) vitiates one of the main benefits that should flow from a National Curriculum, namely, that the teacher knows what can be relied on as having been taught to pupils in the previous year by another teacher, and can build on it efficiently. This aspect is even more important in Britain than on the Continent, since a Continental teacher often teaches the same class of pupils for 2–4 years in succession, whereas in Britain the teacher usually changes each year.

It is taken for granted on the Continent that each pupil has his or her own main textbook for each subject: it is used during part of the lesson; is taken home for homework, advance preparation and revision; and it enables parents to be informed about schoolwork. In England duplicated worksheets are prevalent; they are often taken from a variety of textbooks, or are produced individually by each teacher, and are distributed to each group of pupils according to their varied needs. The system thus reflects the individualistic English teaching emphasis.

Continental teachers' manuals to accompany pupils' textbooks have been developed to a much greater extent than in England. The manuals provide a suggested scheme of lessons for the whole year, outline the main learning objectives of each lesson (or group of lessons for the week) in relation to each page or group of pages in the pupils' text, and provide supplementary teaching material; the manual is not obligatory, but often forms part of a learning scheme approved as covering the obligatory curriculum. In Britain each school is expected to develop its own Scheme of Work (a technical term!) which is supposed to interpret in detail the requirements of the National Curriculum to suit the individual circumstances of each school; the preparation of such a scheme is a laborious task, occasionally carried out by the local education authority together with local teachers on behalf of the schools within its province. British teachers' manuals, insofar as they have been developed, are less detailed and less specific; this is probably because of the difficulties in specifying how the different groups in each classroom are simultaneously to be instructed.

These aspects of British schooling cannot effectively be changed simply by additional legislation on the National Curriculum. Existing teachers have been trained that their main duty and main task is to cope within the same classroom with that great diversity of pupils' attainments which they inherit from their pupils' previous teachers. That diversity is widely regarded as a virtually unchangeable fact of nature. A National Curriculum on Continental lines – with a tighter focus on what should be taught and mastered in each year of schooling by the great majority of pupils – might well be judged by most teachers in Britain as making inadequate allowance for the diversity of attainments in a typical British year-group of pupils.

Changes in classroom organisation and teaching styles to include more whole-class teaching have frequently been recommended by Her Majesty's Inspectorate as an essential element to make better use of learning time; but HMI have been short in analysis and prescription of what is necessary by way of preconditions if teachers are to move in that direction. HMI have not made it clear, for example, whether they recommend more setting or streaming by ability, whether textbooks should be used more systematically, or whether some other steps need be taken; on the whole, they have been critical of schools that relied on a textbook – but without suggesting clear alternatives.

To keep the variability of pupils' attainments within the class in check, much rethinking of many accepted features of British school organisation may be necessary. Starting with entry to primary school: should late-developing children spend an extra year in a nursery or reception class, and enter 'real school' a year later, as in many parts of the Continent? Should supplementary classes be provided in core subjects for lagging pupils, whether during normal schooling hours, at weekends, or during school vacations? Would there be a subsequent net benefit for lagging pupils if they repeated the final year at their primary school, or moved for a year into some type of local interim class – with fewer pupils per teacher – before moving to their intended secondary school? Continental experience suggests that such measures are helpful and minimise the need for any widespread class repetition; but their experience also suggests that the ultimate sanction of class repetition needs to be available to persuade all concerned – pupils, parents and teachers – of the need to maintain standards. Going beyond the confines of each school, it has also to be asked whether detailed coherent schemes of work for each subject – to replace the investment at present made by each school – should be provided centrally to cover the requirements of the National Curriculum – in the way that textbooks and manuals are centrally approved to help Continental teachers. This is a task for the National Curriculum bodies (or perhaps for HMI to provide endorsements of schemes produced commercially). Such matters go well beyond ideas at present embodied in the legislated National Curriculum (and also go beyond the current associated non-statutory exemplification published with the NC); but if schooling in Britain is to become as effective as on the Continent, fresh thought is required at that broader level.

It is arguable that pressures indirectly stoked up by the present National Curriculum may gradually lead to improvements in such organisational matters without the need for explicit intervention. The following example is relevant: for many schools, the major innovation of the National Curriculum was that it was framed in terms of pupils' *attainments* in defined school *subjects*; it consequently has led to moves away from learning through very time-absorbing 'topic work' – which was 'intended to cut across subject boundaries' in the way that 'real life' problems do – and towards more systematic instruction in established subjects and tracking pupils' progress in them. Other changes may also slowly follow as schools experiment with a view to raising their pupils' attainments: but progress would be faster if the underlying problems standing in the way of reforms of classroom organisation and teaching style were faced more explicitly.

Yet other improvements will require an explicit change of emphasis in the legislated National Curriculum. As seen in the previous chapter, certain individualistic features are embodied in the legislated National Curriculum in Britain and absorb disproportionate amounts of school-time. In mathematics, investigatory work – often involving open-ended problems – is required by pupils in Britain, but not on the Continent; in science, pupils' own experiments absorb much more time in Britain than on the Continent, where teachers' demonstrated experiments are regarded as a more efficient way of using learning-time (without excluding a moderate amount of time devoted to pupils' experiments); in practical subjects, pupils in British schools devote much time to their own individual designs, and less to learning the properties of specific materials and the skills necessary to achieve high quality. In response to criticism these aspects have been reduced in the 1994 revision of the National Curriculum, but still remain far from Continental ideas of the efficient use of school-time.

Perhaps the overriding issue relating to preparation for the world of work that requires amendment in the National Curriculum is the provision for practical subjects and technology in the last two years of compulsory schooling (Key Stage 4). At the time of writing, no proposals have been put forward as to how the original National Curriculum is to be modified. The reinstatement of the previous specialised 'single-craft' subjects at GCSE (at present effectively not available for schools in England) is an obvious option; these courses were of good standard, they provided worthwhile attainments in themselves, and they formed a respected foundation for subsequent vocational training.[9] Another option propagated in interested official circles is the incursion into schools of new courses for 14–16-year-olds following the principles which NCVQ has developed for their post-16 qualifications – the Foundation or Intermediate Levels of their *General* National Vocational Qualifications. The NCVQ's lack of experience in what is appropriate for school pupils of that age contrasts with the many decades of experience in this field by the established GCSE school examining boards; there has also been extensive criticism of the content and reliability of those GNVQs which have been tried so far. A third option, in the nature of a compromise with the previous legislated curriculum, is the reduction to a 'half subject' of the requirements for Design and Technology at ages fourteen to sixteen, and for its combination for GCSE examining purposes with the equivalent of a half subject in a single-craft subject (for example, a combined course in motor vehicle studies/design and technology).

Vacillation by the government on what is to be legally obligatory for the last two years of compulsory schooling in this part of the curriculum has obviously had widespread unsatisfactory consequences; it has particularly hindered those schools wishing to develop distinct 'vocational and technical pathways', with a mix of practical and theoretical subjects on the lines of the previous secondary technical schools.

Clearly, much remains to be done. This book will have achieved its purpose if it has stimulated wider understanding and interest in Britain in the experience of its Continental neighbours and, in consequence, contributes to an improved future for British schooling and training systems, and to the widening of Britain's economic and social horizons.

Notes

1 GENERAL PRINCIPLES

1 R. Lowe, *Education in the Post-War Years: A Social History* (Routledge, 1988), p. 57.

2 For related classifications of technology phases, see R.W. Coombs, 'Long-term trends in automation', in P. Marstrand (ed.), *New Technology and the Future of Work and Skills* (Pinter, 1984), especially on the stages within the phase of mechanisation (p. 150).

3 A skilled craftsman in Britain in 1913–14 earned 68 per cent more than an unskilled operative; the differential fell to 49 per cent in 1960 and to only 17 per cent in 1980; since then there has been a recovery to some 30 per cent (for further details, see [3], p. 40).

4 The quotations are from the well-known passage in Adam Smith, *The Wealth of Nations* (Everyman edn, 1910, vol. I, pp. 89f.).

5 J. R. Hicks, *The Theory of Wages* (2nd edn, Macmillan, 1963), p. 320.

6 The technical conditions giving rise to such oscillations are set out in theoretical discussions of so-called Cobweb cycles; these lead to either convergent or divergent cycles, depending on whether the response of supply to higher wages is absolutely greater or less than the response of demand. Maintained oscillations in these cases can arise only if the slopes of the functions are precisely equal; slight variations from that condition, as must occur in practice, would lead to convergence or divergence. More interesting cases involve non-linear (S-shaped) functions, for example, a kinked demand curve, or supply inelastic for small changes but elastic for large changes; these can lead towards a maintained limit-cycle.

7 For the complex dynamics of wage adjustments, see J. R. Hicks, 'The economic foundations of wage policy', *Economic Journal*, 1955, p. 404.

8 These aspects were well illustrated in a study of labour-market forces in three occupations in Britain – draughtsmen, teachers and bus drivers – by B. Thomas and D. Deaton, *Labour Shortage and Economic Analysis* (Blackwell, 1977),

especially p. 210. The shortage of mathematics teachers in Britain is well known; but the employer – effectively the government – has for long been hindered in raising wages in the face of union insistence that fairness requires all teachers' wages (irrespective of subject taught) to rise simultaneously.

9 See G. Becker, *Human Capital* (NBER, Columbia University Press, 1964, 2nd edn 1975), pp. 19–37; policy implications were developed more explicitly by M. Oatey, 'The economics of training', *British Journal of Industrial Relations*, 1970, pp. 13–21. For NIESR studies of this aspect, see I.S. Jones, 'Apprentice training costs in British manufacturing establishments: some new evidence', *British Journal of Industrial Relations*, 1986, p. 333; and 'Training pay and costs of vocational training in Britain and Germany', *Social Forces* (European Commission), 1985. Research on specialised issues has been well summarised by W.S. Siebert, 'Developments in the economics of human capital', chapter 2 of D. Carline *et al.*, *Labour Economics* (Longman, 1985); and, more recently, J. Bishop, *The Incidence of and Payoff to Employer Training*, Cornell University Working Paper 94–17 (July 1994), especially pp. 39–46.

10 See Becker, *Human Capital*, p. 30, with the reference to Marshall's view that the fraction was arbitrary and depended on bargaining; and Siebert, 'Developments', p. 25.

2 PREPARATION FOR WORK IN BRITAIN AND ELSEWHERE

1 This chapter provides a condensed account of a number of earlier detailed National Institute studies, with revisions and updating as necessary. The bibliography at the end of this book lists those studies which have been reproduced in compendia (*Productivity, Education and Training*, NIESR, first volume issued in 1989; a second volume to be issued in 1995). They are referred to here in square brackets according to their chapter number in those compendia (for example [7]). Note that references to Germany in this book relate to the former West German *Länder*.

2 On a stricter categorisation of those with vocational qualifications, making use of more recent information gathered by the Department of Employment, the proportion in Britain with vocational qualifications was estimated at only 25 per cent in 1989 in my Keynes Lecture ([27], table 1). The information on vocational qualifications in Britain is imprecise, but there can be little doubt of the great difference from Germany. More recent information from Germany relating to 1991 (*Mikrozensus*) shows 10 per cent with university qualifications, 61 per cent with vocational qualifications, and 29 per cent with none. Though these relate to the former West German territories, the impact of migrations from former East Germany may have had an impact.

3 Based on the summary figures in *Grund- und Strukturdaten* 1985/86 (p. 95) and 1990/91 (p. 116), with rough adjustments to the *Handwerk* to allow for difference in time units, that column relates to the *flow* of new entrants; to bring it to the same dimension as the other economic sectors shown in that table, which relate to the total *stock* of trainees, it needs to be multiplied by between two and three.

4 The slightly greater proportion of graduates in British than in German manufacturing industry has arisen mainly in the past decade, as appears from the similar table for the latter part of the 1970s shown in the Institute's earlier analysis [1], p. 48.

5 A subsequent comparison for 1990 shows similar contrasts between Britain, on the one hand, and Germany and Switzerland on the other (to appear in a forthcoming analysis of the Swiss system by H. Bierhoff and the present writer). The need to allow for the different qualification systems for teachers (see note 7 below) makes such comparisons not quite as straightforward as might be thought. See also [27].

6 Other comparisons of numbers qualifying in engineering, including qualifications below degree level in Britain, France, Japan and the USA, also point to relatively low numbers in the UK qualifying in engineering (see [14]); numbers graduating in 1976 in Britain and Germany in all subjects were compared in [1], p. 54. In 1987 statisticians at the Department of Education and Science published figures suggesting that in the UK some 15 per cent *more* than in Germany qualify per head of the population in engineering and allied courses in higher education (DES *Statistical Bulletin* 12/90, table 11; and, previously, *Employment Gazette*, December 1987). The difference arose because of a wider, but imprecise coverage by the DES. At first-degree level the DES did not dispute that substantially fewer qualified in the UK. But 'technician' qualifications were included in that DES total, while they excluded the very substantial number qualifying in Germany as *Meister*. This seemed to us a mistake in any realistic international comparison of industry's stock of certified skills at technician level. Because of the substitutability of skills at technician and craft levels, the great German advantage in numbers qualifying at craft level must come into any overall assessment (see [14]); unfortunately the DES study confined itself rather formally to Unesco definitions of 'higher education', and thus excluded the craft category.

7 Strictly, we should at this point take into account differences in the way teachers' qualifications are gained in the two countries; this adds to the complexity of the argument, but without altering the above conclusion, as follows. In Germany, in addition to the degrees enumerated here in table 2.3 (p. 23), some 17,000 teachers' certificates (*Lehramtsprüfungen*) were awarded; in Britain, some 16,000 obtained initial teacher qualifications, of whom 8,000 were non-graduates and 8,000 were graduates (*Education Statistics*, 1989, p. 101). This last number should, strictly, be deducted from the British figures shown in table 2.3 for comparison with the German figures shown here. If we suppose half the graduate teachers had previously acquired degrees in languages and arts, there would still be the very high number of 24,000 with first degrees in these subjects in Britain compared with only 12,000 in Germany.

8 These matters were discussed at some length in the Finniston report, *Engineering Our Future*, Cmnd 7794 (HMSO, 1980), pp. 41, 84, 184. A recent description of the variety of a four-year British engineering course was given by S. Levy 'The integrated engineering programme', in G. Parry (ed.), *Engineering Futures*, 1 (Engineering Council, 1992), pp. 55–66.

9 The decline in numbers qualifying on City and Guilds mechanical engineering courses listed here (course nos. 205, 215, 216, 217) has been drastic – from 16,000 in 1981 to only 3,000 in 1989. Earlier comparisons for 1981 ([2], p. 48) suggested a German advantage by a factor of three for qualified mechanics, based solely on City and Guilds qualifications for Britain. There has been a growing tendency in Britain for engineering apprentices to embark on technician rather than craft qualifications (that is, BTEC rather than C & G), because of the greater range of later options; the initial parts of the technician and craft courses are similar. In the present comparisons in table 2.4 we have therefore also included for Britain estimates of numbers attaining lower-level technician qualifications (BTEC National Certificates and Diplomas); had these been included in our estimates for 1981, the gap would have been shown at a factor of just over two.

10 Including BTEC National in both years (some 7,000 in 1981, added to the C & G total of 12,000 as shown in [2], p. 20), the fall in C & G electrical craft qualifications was about a third (see preceding note).

11 Cf. W.-D. Greinert, *Das 'deutsche System' der Berufsausbildung* (Nomes, Baden-Baden, 1993), p. 21.

12 Note that there is a two-fold distinction: (1) Diplomas have a broader coverage of subjects than Certificates; (2) National level is more advanced than First level, as discussed in the next paragraph (Higher National is above National, and close to a university degree – but that higher level is not of immediate concern here).

13 The breadth of occupational coverage in such international statistical comparisons can be varied (for example, by including banking or insurance clerks), leading to different ratios of persons qualifying in the two countries; alternative calculations that we have carried out indicate that, whichever basis is chosen, the numbers qualifying in Germany are radically greater in Britain.

14 A. Allcock, 'A new era of training', *Machinery and Production Engineering*, 15, February 1991.

15 See *National Institute Economic Review*, February 1989 and May 1991.

16 A German practical test at this level was said by a British teacher, who acted as one of our assessors for electrical tests at City and Guilds part 2 and the German *Berufsabschluss*, to be 'quite beyond' the competence of our trainees ([2], p. 51).

17 For comparisons between the Business Calculations test paper set by BTEC and the German and French corresponding tests, see [2], pp. 58 and 62; and [7], p. 64.

18 *Skills Testing in the Building Industry*, CITB Bulletin no. 3, July 1987.

19 Curiously enough, at the time of this writing, a skilled carpenter has so far made three unsuccessful attempts at rehanging the front door of the National Institute in order that the door should shut properly after he had refixed an automatic door-closer.

20 A brief account of the Rugby experiment, and references to fuller accounts, are given in Appendix E of S.J. Prais, *Productivity and Industrial Structure* (Cambridge University Press, 1981), pp. 294–5.

21 Hessen (largest city, Frankfurt) is now exceptional in not permitting such a substitution in general, and a full legal obligation to attend day-release classes till

eighteen remains as part of general schooling requirements (law of 30 June 1992, s.62(3); exceptions are possible under s.63(2), but require specific permission). Most of those who attend full-time for one year in the rest of Germany are on courses directed towards one of a dozen broad occupational groups (*Berufs-grundbildungsjahr* – BGJ), but some attend wholly general vocational preparation courses (*Berufsvorbereitungsjahr* – BVJ).

22 The following figures for a cohort in successive years broadly illustrate the recent situation. In 1986 there were some 800,000 15-year-olds in Germany; in 1987 some 85,000 attended BGJ and BVJ; in 1988 some 38,000 of the latter group were enrolled in part-time vocational courses (*Grund- und Strukturdaten*, 1988, p. 40; *Bildung und Kultur: 11.3: Berufliche Bildung 1988*, pp. 81 and 92, with adjustment for average length of course).

23 There is a great diversity of educational and vocational standards both among and within the various American states. A recent attempt to compare school-to-work transitions in the USA and Britain by an American scholar decided to ignore (what in Britain are called) Further Education qualifications because, in his view, there was a 'lack of anything in the United States comparable to [the] system of [intermediate vocational] qualifications in Great Britain' (A.C. Kerkhoff, *Getting Started*, Westview Press, 1990, p. 67). An earlier attempt to match qualifications in the USA and Britain, within the framework of the National Institute's series of comparisons, nevertheless deserves noting. It suggested that the US workforce at the end of the 1970s was better endowed with university qualifications (20 per cent of the US workforce at first degree level, compared with 7 per cent in Britain), and also somewhat better endowed with intermediate qualifications (57 compared with 43 per cent) – though the latter admittedly could not be defined in any very satisfactory way; correspondingly, the USA had a lower proportion without qualifications (24 compared with 50 per cent). Four-year US university degrees were treated in that comparison as equivalent to British degrees; anyone with a US High School Diploma, or with 1–3 years of full-time college education, was treated as having an intermediate qualification equivalent to those in Britain lying in the broad range between CSE and HND. This was the best that could be done to match the available sample surveys of qualifications in the two countries (A. Daly, 'Education and productivity: a comparison of Britain and the United States', *British Journal of Industrial Relations*, 1986, p. 252). HMI's recent comparisons concluded that US High School Diplomas were little more than a 'testimony of attendance' and bore little relation to pupil's attainments (*Aspects of Education in the USA: Vocational and Continuing Education*, HMSO, 1990, p. 3); the consequent variability in actual attainments perhaps accounted for the apparently negative relation between the proportion of the workforce with intermediate qualifications and industry's productivity in Anne Daly's study (p. 261).

24 The trades mentioned have over half receiving their CAP after an apprenticeship. Despite the general requirement of full-time schooling till sixteen, apprenticeship can be started in France at fifteen, provided the *troisième* class has been completed; otherwise only at fifteen and a half. A fifth of those receiving the CAP

did so after an apprenticeship; if we combine CAP with BEP, then only one in seven followed the apprenticeship route (*Repères et références statistiques*, Ministère de l'Education nationale, 1990, pp. 181, 225; hereafter referred to as *RRS*).

25 Some candidates in France take both qualifications; the *Annuaire statistique* 1(table F01–10) until 1986 referred to a special enquiry for 1977 showing that approximately 14 per cent should be deducted from the combined total number of qualifications awarded in order to arrive at an estimate of the number of candidates qualifying. That enquiry does not appear to have been repeated; later editions of the *Annuaire* have simply carried a caution about double counting, without indicating its size. In view of the continued growth in BEP qualifications, the overlap has probably increased; in our calculations we have usually deducted some 20 per cent for the purposes of international comparison.

26 Having in mind the higher youth unemployment rates in France in the late 1980s, the Prime Minister Edith Cresson expressed the view that France would benefit from the installation of an apprenticeship system on the German model (*Times Educational Supplement*, 9 August 1991).

27 Pupils who attend CPPN and CPA have mostly already repeated one year of schooling, while those who attend the *classes technologiques* at *collèges* have mostly repeated two years of schooling (derived from *RRS*, 1993, tables 4.6, 4.7 and 5.1).

28 Derived from *RRS*, 1988, p. 49.

29 G. McCulloch, *The Secondary Technical School: A Usable Past?* (Falmer Press, 1989); for a wider historical background see also the essays on *Technical Education and the State since 1850: Historical and Contemporary Perspectives*, P. Summerfield and E.J. Evans (eds) (Manchester University Press, 1990).

30 See [16] p. 49 and n. 24.

31 These remarks on Switzerland are based on research in progress at the Institute by Helvia Bierhoff and myself; an earlier study by Dr H. Hollenstein, who was a Visiting Research Fellow at the National Institute in 1981–2, was circulated as National Institute Discussion Paper no. 54, 'Economic performance and the vocational qualifications of the Swiss labour force compared with Britain and Germany'. At the end of the 1970s Switzerland produced about a quarter more graduate engineers and technologists than Germany per head of the workforce; during the 1980s Germany's expansion of university qualifications in these subjects was greater than in Switzerland, and there was little difference between these two countries by the end of the decade. (I am grateful to Dr Hollenstein for subsequent correspondence on these matters.)

32 The above paragraphs draw mainly on my 1987 study of Japanese schooling and vocational education [13], as well as on the subsequent fuller account of *How the Japanese Learn to Work* by R.P. Dore and M. Sako (Routledge, 1989) and on the recently revised booklet by T. Ishikawa, *Vocational Training* (Japan Institute of Labour, Tokyo, 1987, revised 1991).

33 These figures for Britain and Germany in 1978–80 differ slightly from those shown in table 2.1 above because of slight differences in classification by Dr H.

Hollenstein (of the Swiss Federal Institute of Technology, Zurich) for comparability with Switzerland.

3 PRODUCTIVITY AND ITS DETERMINANTS: CASE STUDIES

1 For consumer durables in the USA, cumulative overestimates of price rises by 1.5 per cent a year, and corresponding underestimates of the growth of real output by the same amount, have been estimated by R.J. Gordon for the period 1947–83; these mis-estimates are the consequence of inadequate adjustment for quality changes by official statisticians there. For producers' durables, the error was estimated to be twice as large, at 2.9 per cent a year for the same period (*The Measurement of Durable Goods Prices*, NBER, University of Chicago Press, 1990). See also the papers by Griliches and Triplett, and especially the sober historical comment by Diewert, in E.R. Berndt and J.E. Triplett (eds), *Fifty years of Economic Measurement*, Studies of Income and Wealth no. 54 (University of Chicago Press, 1990), pp. 185–238.

2 Our research approach contrasts with others where plants that were very much larger (1,000 or more employees) were compared, but where only very few plants were included in the sample. Thus, only three very large plants in each country, with an average of 1,300 employees each, were included in the Anglo-French-German comparisons by Maurice, Sorge, Warner and their associates at the end of the 1970s (see A. Sorge and M. Warner, *Comparative Factory Organisation*, Gower, 1986, pp. 51–4); the Anglo-Japanese comparisons by Dore were based on only two plants in each country with an average of over 2,000 employees per plant (R. Dore, *British Factory, Japanese Factory*, Allen & Unwin, 1973).

3 Comparisons of Censuses of Production for Britain and Germany in 1987 yielded a gap of 31 and 35 per cent for metal products and mechanical engineering respectively; the gap in 1983–4, when the Institute's plant visits were made, was about 12 per cent higher than in 1987 for all manufacturing (see M. O'Mahony, 'Productivity levels in British and German manufacturing industry', *National Institute Economic Review*, February 1992, pp. 50 and 55), suggesting a gap of about 50 per cent for metal trades in 1983–4 .

4 Our US visit yielded similar impressions: the drill bits manufactured there were designed to be of higher precision; and the screws made there were designed for local specialist application.

5 Sir F. Warner, *Standards and Specification in the Engineering Industries* (NEDO, 1977); and the sequel *Progress on the Warner Report* (NEDO, 1980).

6 Both the NEDO report on toolmaking and the paper by Sorge and Warner on mechanical engineering (see note 2) noted fewer managerial staff in Germany than in Britain. Similar findings in comparisons with the Netherlands, Sweden and Japan appeared in reports for NEDO by the Process Plant EDC, *The Challenge from Abroad* (1982), and the Iron and Steel Sector Working Party, *A Hard Look at Steel* (1982). In view of these earlier findings, and the need to keep our interviews short, we did not ask about indirect labour in the comparisons reported above.

7 [16], p. 50. For a detailed account of productivity changes in one very important sector of engineering products – vehicle components – in 1981–2 and 1989–90, see C. Carr, 'Productivity and skills in vehicle component manufacturers in Britain, Germany, the USA and Japan', *National Institute Economic Review*, February 1992, p. 79.

8 [17], p. 62.

9 The difference was statistically highly significant ($t > 5$).

10 See [11], Appendix A for details of the regression analysis. In addition to the factors mentioned above, a dummy variable was included for two hotels suspected by the Institute researchers to be on the grade borderline; but this variable was not found to be statistically significant. Within our limited sample, we could also not detect statistically significant differences between larger and smaller German cities.

11 *The Future of the British Car Industry* (Cabinet Office, HMSO, 1975), p. 84.

12 [9], p. 89. To put the British breakdowns into perspective: there were, say, an average of five main production lines in each factory, of which one was defective. If half the factories exhibited such a defect, and the defect could be repaired in a day, the loss of production for the sample as a whole would be of the order of 10 per cent. This may seem small: but it probably represents only the tip of an iceberg – the part of the maintenance problem most immediately visible to an outside observer.

13 [10], p. 46. The three specific items of machinery mentioned carry out the following functions: (a) starting from a pile of rectangular pieces of material cut to rough size for each garment, the whole pile is cut in a single operation to yield the set of precise component shapes required to make up the batch of garments; (b) where parts of the garment require stiffening, a lining is fused to the outer material, using heat and pressure; (c) the finished garment is sealed in a polythene covering, ready for the sales counter.

14 [17], p. 71.

15 Going back probably to well before 1975: the interest of the CPRS remark of 1975 (quoted above) was that it attempted to quantify a problem that was already recognised at that time.

16 [8], pp. 58–9.

17 Only Japan's stock was younger than Britain's; the detailed analysis is in my article, 'Some international comparisons of the age of the machine stock', *Journal of Industrial Economy*, 1, 1986, pp. 261–77. An earlier comparison showed Britain's stock to be about a year younger than that of the USA; see R.W. Bacon and W.A. Ellis, *The Ages of US and UK Machinery* (NEDO, 1974).

18 [8], p. 54, and [16], p. 53, table 3. Note that the basis of comparison differed between the two dates (percentage of *firms* in 1983–4, of major *machines* in 1990–1; there is no suggestion here that the actual proportion of CNC machinery decreased in that period).

19 For a further discussion see D. Noble, 'Social choice in machine design: the case of automatically controlled machine tools', in H. Mackay, M. Young and J. Benyon (eds), *Understanding Technology in Education* (Falmer, 1991), pp. 13–

40); and Prais, 'Some international comparisons', p. 274.

20 The adequacy of vocational qualifications was an issue in three British public inquiries held towards the end of the 1980s where public safety suffered: the Clapham Junction railway disaster, where the qualifications of those working on signal wiring for railways were questioned; the Kings Cross Underground fire, where no qualified person was on duty; and the sinking of the *Herald of Free Enterprise*, where there were doubts as to the qualifications of those who left open the front bow vehicle door through which the sea duly entered and sunk the ship. These accidents involved very many fatalities, and all took place within a short period; they raised worrying questions – as yet not satisfactorily answered – as to whether skill-certification and associated safety procedures in Britain had by then dropped below a critical level.

21 [10], p. 49.

22 [16], p. 55.

23 See note 20 above.

24 It might be thought that the production-control task in Britain was simpler since long runs of standardised products were made, rather than short runs of individualised designs as in Germany; and that Britain therefore managed very sensibly to get by with personnel having lower levels of qualification. In reality, poor reliability of machinery in Britain, rejects and other problems made the tasks of the British production controller more demanding and exhausting; there were frequent interruptions of routine production to make up shortfalls in ordered quantities, hectic progress chasing – most of which should have been avoided if there had been greater competence of the sort that the German *Meister*-controlled team was required to have.

25 Just one housekeeper in the sample of fourteen British hotels had acquired a vocational qualification – but in another occupation.

26 The principles of work-scheduling in hotels seem simple, but training seems necessary for it to be applied systematically and to reduce surplus waiting time of room staff. In brief: it takes more time (a) to change a room when a guest is leaving than (b) to tidy it if the guest is staying another night; and it takes longer still (c) to give the rooms the occasional thorough 'spring clean' which is necessary if the hotel is to maintain standards. Work-scheduling requires a systematic long-term allocation of type (c) tasks having regard to the immediate requirements of tasks (a) and (b). A 'spring clean' may take more than a day (for example, to allow carpets to dry after shampooing), and thus also requires a forecast by management of the likely degree of room occupancy some days ahead.

27 In total there were sixty-six teams, forty-seven from individual industries and nineteen which dealt with broader cross-industry topics (for example, metal finishing, training of operatives); see *The Final Report of the Anglo-American Council on Productivity* (London, 1952).

28 Not all reports were as explicit on this important aspect as that on the *Training of Supervisors* (1951), p. 4. Even in furniture, where 'small' US plants formed a larger proportion of the total, the median size of plants visited had 1,500 employees (that is, half of all employees in the sample were in plants above that

size and half below; Report on furniture, 1952, p. 2).
29 Report on pressed metal (1950), p. 44; see also the report on valves (1951), pp. 48–9.
30 Pressed metal report, p. 44, and furniture report, p. 63.

4 EDUCATION AND PRODUCTIVITY

1 See T. Husen (ed.), *International Study of Attainments in Mathematics* 2 vols., (Almquist & Wiksell, Stockholm, 1967). Much the same ground was covered by N. Postlethwaite, *School Organisation and Student Achievement: A Study Based on Student Achievement in Mathematics in Twelve Countries* (Wiley, 1967). For an over-critical review, see H. Freudenthal, 'Pupils' achievements internationally compared, published in the journal he edited, *Educational Studies on Mathematics*, vol. 6, no. 2, July 1975. pp. 127–86 (Reidel, Dordrecht, Holland). The original stated aims of the IEA studies may have been only partially achieved, as Freudenthal argued; nevertheless, important lessons are to be drawn from them, especially if successive studies are considered together, and in conjunction with other information. The IEA studies provided invaluable starting points in the National Institute's observations of schools in Britain and the Continent. From the point of view of assessing Britain's schooling performance, it is a matter of concern that Britain's schools did not cooperate as well as other countries to these surveys (a response rate of under half), with a likelihood that weaker schools and weaker pupils were not adequately represented; the true shortcomings of British pupils' attainments are thus likely to be understated in these surveys (see notes 8 and 15 below on Britain's response rate to the 1981 and 1991 surveys).

2 The comparisons in this paragraph are, in reality, even less favourable to England since its Secondary Modern schools accounted for a greater proportion of all pupils than the German *Hauptschulen*; that is, the English pupils on average came from a higher slice of the attainment range than the German pupils in this comparison.

3 See Appendix B of the article by the present writer and Dr Karin Wagner (of the Technical University, Berlin) in the *National Institute Economic Review*, May 1985, for sources and details of adjustments.

4 B. Bloom, 'Implications of the IEA studies curriculum and instruction', chapter 3 in A.C. Purves and D.V. Levine (eds), *Educational Policy and International Assessment* (McCutchan, Berkeley, Calif, 1975), pp. 78–9.

5 R. Marshall and M. Tucker, *Thinking for a Living: Education and the Wealth of Nations* (Basic Books, New York, 1992), esp. pp. 154–5 on the difficulties of using German 'top-of-the-line machines' in the USA because of the inadequate technical training of US operatives. See also I.C. Magaziner *et al.*, *America's Choice: High Skills or Low Wages: Commission on the Skills of the American Workforce* (National Center on Education and the Economy, Rochester, N.Y., 1990).

6 Based on calculations of the variability of pupils' scores in seven of the participating countries prepared by Professor Postlethwaite – then president of the IEA –

for a National Institute conference; see T.N. Postlethwaite, 'The bottom half in lower secondary schooling', chapter 8 in G.D.N. Worswick (ed.), *Education and Economic Performance* (Gower, 1985), p. 94. The comparison of science attainments by the lowest quarter of pupils is derived from chart 8.1 there, and is approximate.

7   *Ibid.*, table 8.1, charts 8.1 and 8.2.

8   From the graphs in chapter 6 (by D.F. Robitaille) in D.F. Robitaille and R.A. Garden (eds), *The IEA Study of Mathematics*, vol. II (Pergamon, 1989) pp. 105, 111, 115, 117, 119. The response rate to this survey in England and Wales was a mere 36 per cent, and very much lower than elsewhere. The details relating to reponse rate are not easily accessible, and may be summarised here. A total of 248 schools were selected for participation in England and Wales, but only 133 cooperated (54 per cent); of the 4,041 pupils in the cooperating schools, only 2,678 were in the achieved sample (66 per cent; see R.A. Garden, *Second IEA Mathematics Study: Sampling Report*, US Department of Education, duplicated 1987, pp. 61 and 88). The consequential possible upward biases in the recorded results for England were not investigated by IEA researchers.

9   The adjustments for age are detailed in my paper in the *National Institute Economic Review*, February 1987, p. 42; and p. 54, note 15.

10   No full investigation of the frequency distribution of scores for the complete set of questions was undertaken on this round by the IEA. For calculations on the anchor items; see M. Cresswell and J. Gubb, *The Second International Mathematics Study in England and Wales* (NFER–Nelson, 1987), p. 66. Additional calculations are available on the basis of a set of forty 'core questions' (to be distinguished from the 'anchor items': the 'core' excluded questions set to various sub-samples of pupils) in Postlethwaite, *Education*, pp. 96–7 (the countries referred to there as B, D, E and F are Sweden, France, Hungary and Japan).

11   The questions in both years were set in multiple-choice form, based on ticking one of five possible answers; the conventional adjustment for guessing has been made here in quoting percentages of those answering correctly; the adjustment is based on the simple assumption that those who did not know the correct answer may have marked it correctly by random ticking. If p is the fraction ticking the correct response, the adjustment required is a deduction of $(1-p)/(n-1)$, where n is the number of possible choices (this follows from assuming that p consists of P, the proportion who really know, plus an equal fraction of the remainder $(1-P)/n$ who are assumed to distribute their ticks at random over the alternatives). This conventional adjustment is subject to fairly obvious limitations; but it seems to me better to quote the results of multiple-choice tests after such an adjustment than without it.

12   Cresswell and Gubb, *Second Study*, pp. 54–64. Not too much attention should be paid to the single question in which English pupils performed statistically 'significantly' better in 1981 since that was an untypical question: even in 1981 a mere 13 per cent of pupils gave the right answer (after adjusting for guessing).

13   Robitaille and Garden, *IEA Study*, vol. II, pp. 160ff.

14   This follows from table 3.27 in Cresswell and Gubb, *Second Study*, p. 66, by

comparing samples of pupils aged 14:1 in 1981 with a suitably weighted average of those who in the 1964 sample (population b) were aged 13:5 and those aged 14:4. Other possible reasons for the decline in performance considered by these authors (pp. 66–7) do not seem important, except for the change in curriculum coverage considered below.

15 A.E. Lapointe, N.A. Mead and J.M. Askew, *Learning Mathematics* (Educational Testing Source, Princeton N.J., 1992), derived from fig. 1.1, p. 18. The response rate in England was a highly unsatisfactory 47 per cent compared with some 80 per cent for France, Switzerland and Italy; on the basis of other studies it seemed likely that low-attaining schools tended not to participate (see, for example, D. Foxman, *Learning Mathematics and Science: The Second International Assessment of Mathematics and Science in England*, NFER, 1992, p. 3 and note 6). NFER subsequently kindly cooperated with our request to compute adjustment factors for response bias based on published GCSE attainments of schools that were approached for the IAEP survey and of those schools that participated; the originally published score for the lowest decile of 34.5 (Lapointe *et al.*, p. 145) was consequently lowered to 32, as quoted in table 4.2 above. There was no other adjustment of any substance. This method of allowing for bias in the results for England can be regarded as only partial for the following reason. Contrary to sampling procedures in other countries (which took a representative sample of pupils throughout the attainment range in each school), procedure in England was based on sampling whole classes; classes in mathematics in English comprehensive schools are usually 'set' on the basis of ability, and it consequently seems likely that there were additional biases within the schools as a result of lower response by low-attaining *classes*. The method of adjustment adopted here accounts, at a guess, for perhaps no more than half the total bias. Because of the much higher response rates in other European countries mentioned, no adjustments of comparable magnitude are needed there.

16 Based on graphical interpolation from summary distribution published by Lapointe *et al.* (see note 15), p. 145. (OECD, *Education at a Glance*, 1992, p. 123, published a curious alternative table which is not wholly consistent with that by Lapointe.)

17 *Mathematics Counts* (HMSO, 1982), para. 342.

18 For example, which number is more than 6,399? The Cockcroft Report says: 'the average child can perform this task at age 11 . . . ', and 'there are *some* 14 year-olds who cannot do it and *some* 7 year-olds who can' (para. 342, my italics); but *some* is not defined. A second comparison quoted by Cockcroft was based on simple fractions: how much is two-fifths of 40, or three-quarters of £24; the former can be answered by the top 15 per cent of 10-year-olds, the latter cannot be answered by the bottom 15 per cent of 14–15-year-olds. The only source quoted in the Report (p. 100) relates to the first question (6,399+1); but the source quoted (K.M. Hart (ed.), *Children's Understanding of Mathematics 11–16*, John Murray, 1981), remarkably enough, does not provide this information (the additional sum was mentioned by Margaret Brown in *ibid.*, chapter 4, p. 49, but not the varying proportions answering correctly according to ability range). The

same sum appeared in M. Ward, *Mathematics and the 10-Year-Old* (Schools Council Working Paper 61, Evans/Methuen, 1979), pp. 74–5, showing that 41–48 per cent of all 10-year-olds can answer correctly; but there was no reference to other ages nor to particular ability levels (I am grateful to Professor Margaret Brown of King's College, London, for help with these sources).

19 *National Curriculum: Task Group on Assessment and Testing: A Report* (Chairman: Professor P.J. Black; DES; undated, c.1988), figure 1, printed between paras. 104 and 105. The notion that all school subjects can be put on to a linear ten-level measuring rod, independent of the age of the pupil, is itself debatable; it perhaps seems more applicable in, say, mathematics and foreign languages than in history or English. But even in mathematics, what should be taught to an advanced 9-year-old is not the same as should be taught to a weak 16-year-old – though on the TGAT scale both would be at Level 4. These fundamental matters were reconsidered by the new School Curriculum and Assessment Authority under Sir Ron Dearing in 1994; at the time of this writing it does not appear that the weaknesses of the TGAT approach have been overcome.

20 On the assumption of a statistically normal distribution, the *six*-year span posited by TGAT for the central 80 per cent of pupils corresponds to only a *five*-year span for the central 70 per cent for which the Cockcroft Committee had posited a seven-year span. There was thus a substantial contraction, as far as official thinking was concerned, from Cockcroft's seven-year to the TGAT five-year span of attainments at age eleven. If there was any new evidence on this, it was not produced.

21 The example is given in Lapointe *et al.*, *Learning Mathematics*, p. 29; it was a multiple-choice question with four alternative answers. The results for each country quoted above are based on unpublished tables kindly supplied by the authors, and have here been adjusted for guessing. For the deficiencies in 1964 of English pupils in arithmetic, see Husen, *International Study*, p. 32, tables 1.7 and 1.8.

22 This was an open question, and no adjustment for guessing was necessary. Foxman remarked (*Mathematics and Science*, p. 17) that even Third World countries participating in the comparisons did better on this question than Britain; however, it must be remembered that many 13-year-olds are not registered at school in some Third World countries (Brazil, China), and the results recorded in such international tests are thus likely to be biased upwards.

23 For further examples, see [12], Appendix A, pp. 73–4. The analysis by attainment-range (carried out by the National Foundation for Educational Research) was based on attainments in all mathematics questions in the APU test taken together, rather than on attainments in *all* subjects – which would be closer to the German basis of streaming pupils. If the latter classification could be carried out, no doubt more than 4 per cent would be found capable of answering that question correctly; but probably not many more.

24 See Foxman, *Mathematics and Science*, p. 13. The previous 1981 study (carried out by IEA) suggested that English pupils performed satisfactorily in geometry;

but that study was marred by a 36 per cent response rate for schools in England and Wales (see note 8 above), even poorer than the 1990 IEAP study, and was therefore likely to have a greater upward bias.

25 There is now a clear contrast between Germany and Britain in school examinations at age fifteen to sixteen: calculators are not permitted at all in, for example, *Hauptschule* leaving examinations in Baden-Württemberg; whereas in Britain they are compulsory at GCSE.

26 G. Howson, 'The Mathematics Curriculum towards the year 2000', (US) *Journal of Mathematical Behavior* (1994), and *Journal of Japanese Society of Mathematical Education* (1993, in Japanese).

27 *Bulletin*, 1968, pp. 68 and 77.

28 A further curiosity is that no intermediate levels are permitted under the law (corresponding to average 10- or 12-year-olds, that is, Levels 3½ or 4½). Under the 1994 revision, Statements of Attainment have been replaced by broader 'Level Descriptions', without changing the worrying vagueness described above. Thus, for the new version of Attainment Target 1 in mathematics: at Level 3, 'pupils show that they understand a general statement by finding particular examples that match it'; at Level 4, 'they search for a pattern by trying out ideas of their own'; and at Level 5, 'they make general statements of their own, based on evidence they have produced, and give an exploration of their reasoning'. These may seem unobjectionable activities but they could as well form part of other subjects (English expression, science!) and not absorb time from the basic arithmetic which pupils need at that age.

29 These issues are discussed further by Alison Wolf, 'Testing investigations', in P. Dowling and R. Noss (eds), *Mathematics versus the National Curriculum* (Falmer, 1990), especially pp. 148–50. See also the Cockcroft report, p. 74. The example on prime numbers derives from a theorem proved, but only partially, by Vinogradof in 1937 (I am indebted to Professor Howson for this information). The term 'realistic' mathematics is due to the late Professor H. Freudenthal of the University of Utrecht (see, for example, his *Revisiting Mathematics Education*, Kluwer, Dordrecht, 1991).

30 'Undemanding time-filling exercises' of this sort have recently been recognised (in those terms) by HMI as a source of unsatisfactory standards (*The Teaching and Learning of Number in Primary Schools*, Ofsted, HMSO, 1993, p. 3); but HMI did not ask themselves why such 'undemanding' tasks are characteristically set more frequently in British than in Continental schools.

31 For example, a qualified motor mechanic routinely needs to be able to carry out divisions, such as divide 600 by 0.2, to set the torque correctly on tools. As we saw on our visits to vocational schools in Britain and the Continent, this kind of calculation is difficult even at age twenty for English final year mechanical students, and consequently leads to intuitive solutions and imprecise work; that calculation was taken in their stride by a corresponding class of vocational pupils on the Continent to whom we set the same exercise, and who had been taught arithmetic at their secondary schools to higher standards. Following representations by the Institute team, the above division sum was included as a specific

example in the National Curriculum revision of 1989 at Level 7, that is, as suitable for pupils aged sixteen – but only for those who are above average in their attainments (say, the top 40 per cent) – while on the Continent, as indicated, this kind of sum is taken in their stride by a much broader cross-section of pupils.

32 Further details may be found in [24].

33 HMI, *Technology Key Stages 1, 2 and 3* (HMSO, 1992), p. 18.

34 The italicised words all form part of NC specification.

35 An earlier version of the following paragraphs was submitted to the House of Commons Education Committee in February 1994 by Roger Luxton (Principal Inspector of Schools in the London Borough of Barking and Dagenham) and the present writer.

36 A 'school-readiness test' is sometimes applied on the Continent before entry to primary school, but usually only as a diagnostic aid to help parents decide – in consultation with teachers – whether it would be better to delay a child's entry to school by a year. Similarly, advanced children may enter a few months earlier than the normal age (for example, four months earlier in Zurich, six months earlier in parts of Germany). A slow-developing child, instead of entering a year later, may be recommended to join a class of younger children who spend two years on what is covered in one year by a parallel class. This initial flexibility in age of entry substantially reduces the subsequent need for class-repetition, and its potential embarrassment. A larger proportion of those who enter primary school a year later are from the younger end of the year-group: instead of being, say, four months below the average age of their 'normal' class, in which they might have difficulties, they enter school a year later in a class in which they are just two months above the normal oldest age – and have a better chance of keeping up with that class's progress.

37 The difference between pupils in a class being an 'audience' and being 'participants in sustained interaction' is pointed out in a recent critical essay on current British teaching methods by C. Gipps (*What we Know about Effective Primary Teaching*, University of London Institute of Education, Tufnell Press, 1992, p. 20); the cumulative longer-term benefits of the latter teaching style for pupils' learning attainments, as evident from Continental teaching practice, were not however developed in her essay.

38 When Mr B. Samuelson, MP, visited schools in Switzerland and adjacent parts of Germany over a hundred years ago, he reported to Parliament that schooling there is regarded 'by the children themselves, rather as a pleasure than a duty. The hours which I spent attending the classes of the Volksschulen of Winterthur, of Stuttgart, and of Crefeld, will long remain in my memory as the most delightful incidents of my journey. The lessons consisted of *animated exercises and conversations, in which the teachers and pupils joined with equal zest. The attention of the youngest and least intelligent scholar never flagged for an instant.* Nowhere else is the art of developing and informing the minds of young children understood and practised in such perfection . . .' (House of Commons papers, *Technical Education in Various Countries Abroad*, 26 November 1867, p. 37, my emphasis). Mr Samuelson subsequently chaired the well-known Commission

of Inquiry into schooling of 1881–4. Current classroom practice in Japan and China is much more similar to current Continental than Anglo-American practice (H.W. Stevenson and J.W. Stigler, *The Learning Gap*, Summit Books, New York, 1992).

39 Remarkably enough, up to 'four different activities undertaken at any one time' in a single class was still considered as manageable by HMI writing in 1993, even after reports by the 'three wise men' and by the NCC advocating more whole-class teaching (see R. Alexander, J. Rose and C. Woodhead, *Curriculum Organisation and Classroom Practice in Primary Schools: A Discussion Paper*, DES, 1992; National Curriculum Council, *The National Curriculum at Key Stages 1 and 2*, NCC, January 1993; and Ofsted, *Curriculum Organisation and Classroom Practice in Primary Schools: Follow-up Report*, DFE, 1993, para. 9). One of our colleagues observed *eleven* different activities proceeding simultaneously in a class of 7-year-olds.

40 Detailed studies by Professor Maurice Galton and his colleagues on pupils' use of time in English classrooms indicate that, despite the intensive emphasis on individualised learning, for 80 per cent of the lesson time the average pupil was interacting neither with a teacher nor with another pupil, but was working on his or her own, or waiting for attention. The teacher spent 80 per cent of the time with individual pupils but each pupil received, of course, only a small fraction. Negligible time was spent by the teacher in addressing groups of pupils (rather than individual pupils). Most of the interaction between pupil and teacher came from the 20 per cent of the lesson when the teacher addressed the whole class – and much of that dealt with organisational matters. These studies by Professor Galton are summarised in his *Teaching in the Primary School* (Fulton, 1987), p. 45; and by Gipps, *What we Know*, p. 11.

41 The serious difficulties of teaching under the English individualistic approach, even in the first years of primary school, were investigated by Professor Bennett and his colleagues in the early 1980s. As a particular criticism, they noted that slower pupils suffered because they were given insufficient time to practise what lay within their capacities, while faster pupils spent too much time practising what they had mastered and were not given sufficient fresh topics (N. Bennett, C. Desforges, A. Cockburn and B. Wilkinson, *The Quality of Pupil Learning Experiences*, Lawrence Erlbaum, 1984). In principle, these difficulties, of course, arise in classes everywhere; but I suspect they have become more serious in England because of the lack of emphasis on teaching at an early age in such a way that the whole class advances together. Research in the United States in the past twenty years has confirmed the benefits which slower pupils receive from forms of instruction similar to the Continental methods described above (see B. Rosenshine and R. Stevens, 'Teaching functions', chapter 13 in M.C. Wittrock (ed.), *Handbook of Research on Teaching*, 3rd edn, Macmillan New York, 1986).

42 For example, the Federal Swiss guidelines on mathematics emphasise mental arithmetic throughout obligatory schooling. The objects are stated to be: to 'automate understanding through experience', and to gain speed by 'increasing

mental work and minimising written work' (*Treffpunkte und Richtlinien*, EDK, Geneva, 1982, p. 16). The notion that many pupils learn ideas and procedures more effectively by explaining them orally to others, and to do so as a structured part of a lesson, is supported by psychologists' studies of early childhood (as mentioned by Gipps, *What we Know*, p. 4). The oral method of learning must, however, not be over-stressed at later ages. Taken to extremes, it can easily encourage that lack of conciseness and verbal indiscipline characteristic of American children; some psychologists regard thinking as no more than suppressed talking, and give inadequate weight to the social and individual advantages resulting from such suppression.

43 Most Swiss schools are conducted on a yet smaller scale and on a very different organisational pattern. Briefly: pupils are allocated to a particular teacher for a period of three years, and that group of pupils forms that teacher's 'class' throughout that period; a number of such classes are accommodated in a school building, but there is no 'head teacher' as such. Administrative responsibilities are carried out to a greater extent by the local education authority, and partly by one of the teachers who is elected to carry domestic responsibilities for a few years at a time. From the point of view of the individual pupil, the school has an organisational framework of a much smaller and more intimate scale than in Britain.

44 Details are given in a companion report by V. Jarvis, [26].

5 FROM PRINCIPLES TO PRACTICE

1 (Taunton) Schools Inquiry Commission, vol. 1, *Report of the Commissioners*, 1868, pp. 78–80. Earlier visits to the Continent, starting in the 1830s, had been undertaken for the educational authorities by Sir James Kay-Shuttleworth and are reported in his *Four Periods of Public Education* (Longman, 1862); see especially pp. 211–21, 341–5.

2 Ninth (variorum) edn of Alfred Marshall's *Principles of Economics* (ed. C.W. Guillebaud, Macmillan for the Royal Economic Society, 1961), vol. II, pp. 307–8.

3 A. Marshall, *Industry and Trade* (Macmillan, 1919; 4th edn 1923), pp. 130–1.

4 The experimental introduction of obligatory day release in Rugby in 1920 is described in Appendix E of S.J. Prais *et al.*, *Productivity and Industrial Structure* (Cambridge, 1981), pp. 294–5.

5 For a full historical account, see Correlli Barnet, *The Audit of War* (Macmillan, 1986); a shorter survey is available in the opening chapter of D.H. Aldcroft, *Education, Training and Economic Performance 1944 to 1990* (Manchester University Press, 1992). The detailed observations of Continental schooling and training by nineteenth- and early twentieth-century investigators, and the differences they noted from Britain, provided valuable guideposts for the international comparisons by the National Institute in the past decade reported in this book.

6 Towards the end of 1994 the government's inspectorate joined many previous critics of NCVQ. Among official criticisms, it is sufficient here to mention the

Chief Inspector of Further Education who, in his *Annual Report for 1993–4*, noted the need for NCVQ to provide 'greater clarification of the knowledge, understanding and core skills requirements of each NVQ before accreditation'; and further steps are needed 'if NVQs are to have vocational credibility'. In relation to GNVQs, the report refers to poor 'pre-enrolment guidance' leading to 'drop-out rates in some colleges [of] more than 50 per cent', and 'inadequately briefed verifiers who pay insufficient attention to standards' (*Quality and Standards in Further Education*, Further Education Funding Council, 1994, pp. 58–9).

7 See note 4 above on a previous two-year requirement in Britain.

8 See note 6 above on drop-out rates.

9 Curiously enough, under the 1994 version of the National Curriculum in Design and Technology, 'In Wales, there are no statutory requirements at Key Stage 4' (proof copy circulated to schools, November 1994, p. 10). Welsh schools are therefore free to teach practical subjects in whatever form they prefer; and the Welsh GCSE board is developing further its syllabuses corresponding to the previous specialised single-craft practical subjects.

References and further reading

Many of the detailed research studies underlying the present book were originally published as separate articles in the *National Institute Economic Review* (*NIER*) as each phase of research was completed. For convenience of reference these articles have been photocopied and reissued in two accompanying volumes (available from the publications department, National Institute of Economic and Social Research, 2 Dean Trench Street, London SW1P 3HE). References to such articles are shown in the main text in square brackets; articles [1] to [15] are in the first volume, articles [16] to [27] are in the second volume. Titles of the articles, their authors and place of publication, are as follows:

[1] Vocational qualifications of the labour force in Britain and Germany, by S.J. Prais, *NIER*, November 1981.

[2] Some practical aspects of human capital investment in training standards in five occupations in Britain and Germany, by S.J. Prais and K. Wagner, *NIER*, August 1983.

[3] Productivity and management: the training of foremen in Britain and Germany, by S.J. Prais and K. Wagner, *NIER*, February 1988.

[4] Vocational training in France and Britain: mechanical and electrical craftsmen, by H. Steedman, *NIER*, November 1988.

[5] Vocational training in France and Britain: the building trades, by S.J. Prais and H. Steedman, *NIER*, May 1986.

[6] Vocational training in France and Britain: office work, by H. Steedman, *NIER*, May 1987.

[7] Two nations of shopkeepers: training for retailing in France and Britain, by V. Jarvis and S.J. Prais, *NIER*, May 1989.

[8] Productivity, machinery and skills in a sample of British and German manufacturing plants: results of a pilot enquiry, by A. Daly, David M.W.N. Hitchens and K. Wagner, *NIER*, February 1985.

[9] A second look at productivity, machinery and skills in Britain and Germany, by H. Steedman and K. Wagner, *NIER*, November 1987.

[10] Productivity machinery and skills: clothing manufacture in Britain and Germany, by H. Steedman and K. Wagner, *NIER*, May 1989.

[11] Productivity and vocational skills in services in Britain and Germany: hotels, by S.J. Prais, V. Jarvis and K. Wagner, *NIER*, November 1989.

[12] Schooling standards in England and Germany: some summary comparisons bearing on economic performance, by S.J. Prais and K. Wagner, *NIER*, May 1985; and *Compare: A Journal of Comparative Education*, 1986, no. 1.

[13] Educating for productivity: comparisons of Japanese and English schooling and vocational preparation, by S.J. Prais, *NIER*, February 1987; also in *Compare: A Journal of Comparative Education*, 1986, no. 2; and (in translation) in the *Japanese Journal of Vocational Education*, November 1988.

[14] Qualified manpower in engineering: Britain and other industrially advanced countries, by S.J. Prais, *NIER*, February 1989.

[15] How Europe would see the new British initiative for standardising vocational qualifications, by S.J. Prais, *NIER*, August 1989.

[16] Vocational education and productivity in the Netherlands and Britain, by G. Mason, S.J. Prais and B. van Ark, *NIER*, May 1992.

[17] Productivity, product quality and workforce skills: food processing in four European countries, by G. Mason, B. van Ark and K. Wagner, *NIER*, February 1994.

[18] Innovation and the skill mix: chemicals and engineering in Britain and Germany, by G. Mason and K. Wagner, *NIER*, May 1994.

[19] Vocational qualifications in Britain and Europe: theory and practice, by S.J. Prais, *NIER*, May 1991.

[20] Financing training in Britain, by P.E. Hart and A. Shipman, *NIER*, May 1991.

[21] Shifting foundations: the impact of NVQs on youth training for the building trades, by H. Steedman and J. Hawkins, *NIER*, August 1994.

[22] Improvements in workforce qualifications: Britain and France 1979–83, by H. Steedman, *NIER*, August 1990.

[23] Intermediate skills in the workplace: deployment, standards and supply in Britain, France and Germany, by H. Steedman, G. Mason and K. Wagner, *NIER*, May 1991.

[24] Britain's industrial skills and the school-teaching of practical subjects: comparisons with Germany, the Netherlands and Switzerland, by H. Bierhoff and S.J. Prais, *NIER*, May 1993.

[25] Note of Dissent to the Interim Report of the National Curriculum Mathematics Working Group, by S.J. Prais, December 1987.

[26] Smoothing the transition to skilled employment: school-based vocational guidance in Britain and Continental Europe, by V. Jarvis, *NIER*, November 1994.

[27] Economic performance and education: the nature of Britain's deficiencies, Keynes Lecture in Economics read at the British Academy, by S.J. Prais, *Proceedings of the British Academy*, 1993.

Index

THE NATIONAL INSTITUTE OF
ECONOMIC AND SOCIAL RESEARCH
PUBLICATIONS IN PRINT

published by
THE CAMBRIDGE UNIVERSITY PRESS
(available from booksellers, or in case of difficulty from the publishers)

ECONOMIC AND SOCIAL STUDIES

XXXI   *British Economic Policy, 1960–74*
        Edited by F.T. BLACKABY. 1978. pp. 472.
XXXV   *Unemployment: a Problem of Policy*
        By G.D.N. WORSWICK. 1991. pp. 297.
XXXVI   *Macroeconomic Policy in Britain 1974–87*
        By ANDREW BRITTON. 1991. pp. 381.

OCCASIONAL PAPERS

XLIV   *Lone Parenthood. An Economic Analysis*
        By JOHN F. ERMISCH. 1991. pp. 209.
XLV   *International Financial Markets. The Performance of Britain
and its Rivals*
        By ANTHONY D. SMITH. 1992. pp. 206.
XLVI   *Productivity and Growth. A study of British Industry 1954–86*
        By NICHOLAS OULTON and MARY O'MAHONY. 1994. pp. 344.
XLVII   *The Single Market Programme as a Stimulus to Change. Comparisons
between Britain and Germany*
        By DAVID MAYES and PETER HART with DUNCAN MATTHEWS and ALAN
SHIPMAN. 1994. pp. 264.

OTHER PUBLICATIONS BY CAMBRIDGE UNIVERSITY PRESS

*The UK Labour Market. Comparative Aspects and Institutional
Developments*
Edited by RAY BARRELL. 1994. pp. 266.
An Economist among Mandarins. A Biography of Robert Hall
By KIT JONES. 1994. pp. 256.

THE NATIONAL INSTITUTE OF
ECONOMIC AND SOCIAL RESEARCH

publishes regularly

THE NATIONAL INSTITUTE ECONOMIC REVIEW

A quarterly analysis of the general economic situation in the United Kingdom and overseas with forecasts eighteen months ahead. The last issue each year usually contains an assessment of medium-term prospects. There are also in most issues special articles on subjects of interest to academic and business economists.

Annual subscriptions, £80.00 (UK and EU) and £100.00 (rest of world), also single issues for the current year, £25.00, are available direct from NIESR, 2 Dean Trench Street, Smith Square, London, SW1P 3HE.

Subscriptions at a special reduced price are available to students and teachers in the United Kingdom on application to the Secretary of the Institute.

Back numbers and reprints of issues which have gone out of stock are distributed by Wm. Dawson and Sons Ltd, Cannon House, Park Farm Road, Folkestone. Microfiche copies for the years 1961–89 are available from EP Microform Ltd, Bradford Road, East Ardsley, Wakefield, Yorks.

Published by
SAGE PUBLICATIONS LTD
(Available from Sage and from booksellers)

ECONOMIC CONVERGENCE AND MONETARY UNION IN EUROPE
Edited by RAY BARRELL. 1992. pp. 288. £35.00 (hardback), £12.95 (paperback) net.

ACHIEVING MONETARY UNION IN EUROPE
By ANDREW BRITTON and DAVID MAYES. 1992. pp. 160. £25.00 (hardback), £9.95 (paperback) net.

MACROECONOMIC POLICY COORDINATION IN EUROPE:
THE ERM AND MONETARY UNION
Edited by RAY BARRELL and JOHN D. WHITLEY. 1993. pp. 294. £37.50 (hardback), £14.95 (paperback) net.